Finding Strength in
Numbers:

The Power of Collective Healing in Communities

ALAN BLACKSHAW

Finding Strength in Numbers
© Alan Blackshaw 2024

ISBN: 978-1-923163-27-0 (Paperback)

A catalogue record for this work is available from the National Library of Australia

Cover Design: Alan Blackshaw and Clark & Mackay
Format and Typeset: Clark & Mackay
Published by Alan Blackshaw and Clark & Mackay

Proudly printed in Australia by Clark & Mackay

CONTENTS

CONTENTS

SECTION 1:

Trauma—
A Layman's Explanation

From the start, I want to put things in simple English. I am not a neuroscientist or a psychologist when it comes to trauma. I am a layman. My background is in community development. Working in the community, it is inevitable that you will encounter people whose lives have been impacted by trauma. This has led me to try to understand trauma, the power it can hold for the person and how we can heal from it. To understand some of the complex information about how we develop, I needed it in simple terms without diluting or misrepresenting the data presented. I'm confident that if I need information in simple terms, others will also require the information to be presented in the same way.

This is not a self-help book on overcoming your trauma. There are already many readily available. Instead, this book focuses on community as where we heal from trauma. It examines why and how we can create this healing community. It is written for people who want to create a stronger and more connected local community. There is an understanding that in doing this, trauma and its effects will be found but that by building local community, the healing of this trauma and its impact has commenced.

We are embarking on a journey from a brief discussion about the nature of trauma to setting the scene and a much more comprehensive discussion about community as our healing place.

Our first stop in our journey is to look at how trauma can impact the development and architecture of our brains, physical health, mental health, psychological wellbeing and many long-term individual and social outcomes.

Introduction

My father was a veteran of the Second World War. During the war, he met and married my mother.

When he returned from the war in the Pacific in 1946, they bought a block of land and built their own home in the country town where their families lived. He was a fitter and turner by trade and worked for the state government-owned rail service as his father had. My mother worked as a secretary and receptionist.

They tried to start a family for the next decade but were unsuccessful. They suffered the disappointment and traumas of miscarriages and one stillbirth. They then decided to adopt a child, and in December 1957, I was adopted by my parents.

At the time of my adoption, I had been in state care for two-and-a-half months. I was born due to a relationship my natural mother had while her partner was away working. When her partner discovered she was pregnant, they decided to put the child up for adoption. Following the adoption, my biological mother and partner were to be married. When it came time for my birth, they drove to the nearest public hospital, where she gave birth and gave me up for adoption. She and her partner returned home the next day, telling their family and friends they had "lost" the baby.

Two-and-a-half years later, my mother had another miscarriage. While she was in hospital for treatment for the miscarriage, another woman was giving birth to a child she would put up for adoption. My parents arranged a private legal adoption of this child. Now, they had two children in their care. A year-and-a-half later, my mother fell pregnant and success-fully gave birth to a child. Her family was now complete. She had three children that she and her husband loved.

From my memory, the three of us had an idyllic childhood. By the time we had come along, my father had left the railway and was working as a boiler attendant at the local hospital. This meant he was around more often to care for his family. We holidayed as a family each year. My parents had the support of my maternal grandmother, who lived a street away. They had an active social life involving regular home-cooked meals and card nights with close friends.

However, as the years went by, it became evident that all was not well with my father. To the outside world, he was a man with a quick wit exhibited through dry humour. At home, he became increasingly silent and was harbouring anger. The stress of shift work at the hospital and running a small business installing and servicing wood-fired and oil heaters contributed to this. Unresolved conflict and trauma lay just below the surface.

He was a man of his generation. In many ways, he was a stereotypical Anglo/Celt. He kept much to himself and did not seek help with any issues he may be experiencing. He was a strong working-class man, proud of his values and a "man's man". For his generation, seeking help with underlying mental health conditions was not done. Of course, keeping things to himself and suppressing problems led to other outcomes. Headaches, high blood pressure, nose bleeds, being a workaholic and absent parent, and having a fiery temper. His temper was never exhibited physically but through words. And he was good with words. At home, we felt like we were walking on eggshells.

My mother saved her children from the worst of his moods. She was incredibly gifted at being our protector, a buffer against the worst of the stress of the household.

Eventually, this unresolved household stress led to verbal clashes between me and my father, with our relationship being rocky at best. The teenage years are often complicated. I can certainly vouch for that. The healing of the relationship only began when he was in hospital following a series of strokes. His final months were when I spent long hours with him, often into the early morning, calming him so he could get some rest. Usually, the hospital would call me, saying he was asking for me and that I seemed to be the only person who could calm him down. These were precious times.

The final healing only came a decade-and-a-half later when my mother was in hospital. She had been given two weeks to live and wanted to ensure everything was sorted out for her children. She told us a story about having letters from a mysterious pen pal in a shoebox. The shoebox was kept in the linen cupboard at our family home. While reviewing her papers, she wanted her children to find these letters before others. She emphasised that these were letters from a "pen friend" she had during the Second World War and didn't want people to get the wrong impression about the relationship between her and this mysterious writer. Of course, we raced home, found the shoebox and took it to the hospital. In the shoebox, we found all the letters my father had written to my mother from New Guinea and Borneo. These were beautiful and touching love letters. My mother gave us the most extraordinary healing gift in this final gesture. She gave us back our father, whom we had lost to his internal battles. He was a loving, considerate man looking for a brighter future.

This one act went a long way in healing our past.

My aunt had told me that my father was a different man before he had gone to war. In retrospect, he suffered from what we now know as post-traumatic stress disorder (PTSD). Something that was just not diagnosed when he was suffering. He rarely spoke about the war. And when he did, it was always some humorous tale. He could never share, even briefly, his pain, so he never found the healing he craved from the trauma. The suppression of his trauma only made it harder for him and those closest to him.

The difficulty is that his trauma became my trauma. Although I did not know his wartime experience, his response to trauma meant that I became traumatised through his behaviours. He was an absent parent. I was emotionally neglected. He was angry and displayed this anger through cutting words. I was emotionally abused. This added to the trauma I had experienced before being adopted due to my natural mother's stressful pregnancy and being left in state care for over two months during an essential period in child and brain development. But my trauma is my trauma. It is not their fault.

They were doing their best to cope with the cards life had dealt them using what they had available to them. My natural mother and adopted father should not be held accountable for my trauma. This is for me to deal with.

I was fortunate. My mother provided a valuable emotional buffer that supported me and my siblings through the worst of my father's trauma. I found my community where I could find healing with others. I had a close group of peers. We had gone through school together. We had found music and the arts together. We had fun together. We were close. And half a lifetime later, we are still friends. My community of friends were a valued component in my journey of healing. I also had a faith community providing me with support and healing. My local church, its youth group and our activities provided bonding and a strong support network. I also found comfort and healing in an intentional community I visited while at college. Here, I found acceptance and further healing. This healing journey continues all these years later. It has included formal and informal support, but always at the centre has been the power of social connection of the community to be our place of healing from trauma. To quote a hackneyed expression, "The answer is always community."

CHAPTER 1:

Our Amazing Brain

We are an incredible species. We are resilient. At the same time, we can be vulnerable and brought to our knees by the most minor things. We can be loving and generous, and we can be violent and heartless. Complex and simple. But there is one constant, and that is change. Our bodies are constantly changing as we grow and age. Our brains never stop changing in response to the world around us.

From conception, we grow from one cell into a fully formed human baby around nine months later. Our mother's body provides us with the protection we need so that at birth, although vulnerable, we are ready to face the world outside.

It sounds simple, but we all know getting to the point of being born can be difficult for the baby and the baby's parents. The stress a woman experiences during pregnancy can impact the developing child. Stress produces hormones. When the mother releases stress hormones, these will be absorbed by the developing baby through the placenta. These hormones affect the mother and the baby's developing central nervous, limbic and autonomic systems.[1]

Brains are Built

Our brains don't come ready-made at birth. Like the rest of our body, it has developed enough for survival and for us to respond to our environment. More complex brain circuits are built on these simpler and more ancient parts of the brain. However, for the brain to develop to its full capacity, it needs the support of adults around the child. Children cannot build the brain architecture by themselves. They need the support of loving carers. Providing caring and attentive support ensures children have the framework for the best start in life. This support begins before birth and continues throughout childhood and adolescence. But, in particular, the first two years of life are vital.

As we grow, the brain continues to develop and continues to be built. How this occurs is not determined solely by our genetic makeup or the experiences we have. It is not a question of "nature versus nurture" but a mixture of both. It is more than our genes. It also involves the environment we live in and our life experiences. In short, nature has its role, and significantly, so do the experiences we have in life. In some ways, it is a bit like a piece of "flatpack" furniture but one where the design can change due to our experiences. For the brain to thrive, the child will need the support and guidance of a caregiver to counter the "storm damage" of the stresses encountered in our daily lives.

When we are born, our brains are in a very early stage of development. The brain stem is fully developed, but much of the rest of the brain is still forming. The brain stem is the part of the brain that contains the nerves connecting the brain with the rest of our body.[2] This connection is a highway enabling us to walk, talk and chew gum.

The Limbic System

An essential part of the brain to develop is the limbic system. This part of our brain lies deep in our brains. It is a network responsible for emotions and memories. The limbic system is all about survival. You may have heard of the term "fight or flight". The limbic system is where this happens. When faced with a threatening situation, the limbic system will spring into operation and alert us of the threat of danger. For those old enough to remember, this is a bit like the robot in *Lost in Space* warning the main character of approaching risk: "Danger Will Robinson, danger", and we will want to run from the threat or fight the menace. For this to occur, the limbic system releases stress hormones (cortisol and adrenaline) into our brains. Our breathing becomes rapid. Our reactions are sharper. We have the energy to spring into action. To run or to fight. This limbic system is part of the most ancient part of our brain and is sometimes referred to as our "caveman brain".[3]

The brain's capacity to overrule the urge to fight or flight is a later intellectual development. At this early stage of development, the brain is designed for survival. Spending time deciding if the lion will attack you could mean the difference between life and death.

When the limbic system is activated, stress hormones such as cortisol and adrenaline are released into our system to give us the energy to either flee the situation or fight. As the rest of our brain develops, we learn to moderate our response to potentially harmful conditions. Even when the higher cognitive functions of our brain are in place, the limbic system will always kick in first when a threat appears. Our later-developed intellectual processes can help us to decide whether we need to respond or ignore the threat the limbic system has identified.[4] In other words, our emotional response comes first. We can use logic to moderate this initial emotional response when cognitive functions develop.

Brain Plasticity

Our brains continue to grow and change throughout our lives. It was once thought that once we became adults, our brains would stop changing, but we now know this is not the case. Our brains continue to grow and change throughout our lives. Every experience we have will cause a change in our brains. We never stop learning and our brain never stops changing. This feature of the brain is called brain plasticity. Every experience we have results in our brain rewiring itself in response to the experience.

There are periods in our lives when the brain develops much quicker than at other times. These are periods when the brain plasticity is most apparent.

The first period of rapid brain growth is in the first year of life. This is the period when the child is most vulnerable to harm. It is also the time when the connections between the components of the brain are most frantic and when the most significant period of change occurs. During this period, a loving, responsive caregiver is essential. Such a caregiver and their supportive actions help the child understand where a fight or flight action is needed or when such a response is unnecessary. For example, a baby will cry. A parent will respond by changing a wet nappy. The child settles down again. For the child, the damp nappy was a source of discomfort and the limbic system sprang into action. The response of the parent showed that this was not a significant threat. The child learns that crying produces a result of someone coming to support them and removing the discomfort and danger. The interaction between the caregiver and the child is critical at this stage.

It can be as simple as a baby smiling and a caregiver returning the smile. Or a child and parent exchanging "baby talk". The Alberta Wellness Initiative labels this as "serve and return". The baby serves up the interaction. The caregiver returns the serve. This positive reinforcement of behaviour, facial expressions and other support can enhance the development of the brain and make the child feel safe in the presence of the caregiver. It provides the best environment for the brain to develop. Without this interaction or if trauma is present, the development is interrupted. It can have adverse impacts on the future development of the child.

Another critical period of brain development is around the time of puberty. This is another time when hormones are "flooding" our brains and other body organs. It is a period of growth and change.

Following this period, brain development will slow down. We only have a developed adult brain in our late 20s. This explains why young people take dangerous risks and why most grow out of this period and settle down to more sedate lifestyles without such a high degree of risk.

In short, our brains change throughout our lives. Brains respond to our environment and our experiences. The most significant times of change are the early years of life and puberty, but our brain continues to change throughout life. It's essential to build a strong foundation in early childhood, beginning before birth. Children need the help of those around them to build strong brains.

It is important to remember that while our brains continue to change, neural pathways are well established in early adulthood, making the "rewiring of the brain" a difficult, but not impossible, task later in life. Try ridding yourself of a well-established habit. It can be done, but it takes some effort.

Trauma

The word "trauma" comes from the Greek word for wound. If we are talking about a trauma a person has experienced, we are not necessarily talking about the incident but the impact that incident has on the person. In the words of Gabor Maté, "It is not the blow on the head, but the concussion I get."[5] This wound can come from an isolated event or ongoing abuse. Trauma can happen at any time in our lives. It can occur in adults and children. But when trauma is experienced when our brains are developing and growing, it can have a lasting impact. It may affect many areas of our lives. This will include our behaviour, learning, physical health, mental health and potential criminality.

Let's look at trauma, stress's role and how it impacts brain development.

CHAPTER 2:

Stress and Brain Development

Before moving on, let's recap what we have said. At birth, our brains are at an early stage of development. What we experience influences how our brains are structured. How our brain is structured can impact our body and life outcomes. We will talk more about those impacts later in this chapter. A significant factor at play in the development of the brain is stress. We all experience stress in our lives. It is a part of our daily life. It can weaken or strengthen us and significantly affect our brain's development.

We experience stress when we encounter fearful or intimidating situations. When this happens, our body releases stress hormones to help us cope with threatening situations. These hormones create the feeling of fight or flight. This is part of our survival instinct. We are set on edge, ready to fight or escape. It is a normal response to stress or danger. However, when these hormones are activated for too long or are present in excessive quantities, our brain, other organs and other bodily systems can be damaged.

But not all stress is bad for us. Sometimes, it can be beneficial. It can be positive, tolerable or toxic. The impact is determined by the duration and intensity of the activation of the stress response, the release of hormones and the support we receive from caregivers.

Positive Stress

Positive stress is a part of normal, healthy development. This type of stress produces a brief increase in the heart rate and mild release and elevation of stress hormones. The presence and support of caregivers buffer this stress. The presence of supportive caregivers ensures the duration of the stress is short. These episodes teach the body and brain how to prepare and cope with future stressful events. This creates a sense of mastery over the event.

Examples of potentially stressful incidents are being dropped off at school, losing a sporting game or meeting new people.

Tolerable Stress

This is a much higher level of stress. It is not good for brain development but will not do any lasting damage if there is buffering support from adult caregivers such as parents.

The type of event that causes tolerable stress is a major life event such as the loss of a family member, important examinations, discrimination or a major accident. Suppose the support of a caregiver is not available. In that case, the raised stress hormone levels will remain in place and become a toxic stress event. The impact of a tolerable stress event can be more or less severe depending on the relationships a person has, their environment and their prior experiences.

Toxic Stress

Toxic stress is an intense, repeated and prolonged response to stressful events. As with tolerable stress, these are significant stressful events, but with toxic stress, there is no adult caregiver who can bring comfort, support the child and teach coping skills. Unlike tolerable stress, where a caring adult will soothe and comfort the child while teaching coping skills, the absence of a caregiver will leave the child with an elevated stress level.

This type of stress is damaging. It is detrimental to the architecture of the brain. It weakens this architecture. The hormones also impact the development of other organs in the body and threaten the child's wellbeing. This can increase the risk of physical and mental illness later in life. In short, it disrupts the brain's development and increases lifelong health risks.

Toxic stress can damage brain development to the extent that the necessary brain architecture required to develop more complex skills may be absent. This can mean the child will not develop integrated cognitive, social and emotional skills. The child could have trouble regulating emotional responses. They may also need help being attentive, need more planning skills, have poor conflict resolution skills and be unable to follow rules and regulations.

This type of stress can involve physical, sexual or emotional abuse, neglect, domestic violence and poverty.

Adverse Childhood Experiences

Adverse childhood experiences (ACEs) are traumatic events and experiences that release dangerously high levels of stress hormones in the body. An ACE may represent one particular event or continuing trauma in a child's life. This is toxic stress in action.

Let's look a little deeper at these types of negative experiences. Toxic stress can impact the development of the brain, the stress response and the development of other organs in such a way as to affect future health, wellbeing and mental health outcomes for the person.

But what exactly are these experiences that generate toxic stress and how common are they?

When a child is subjected to adverse childhood experiences, toxic stress occurs. This type of stress can damage the developing brain and body of the child. In turn, this stress may prevent a child from learning or playing in a healthy way with other children and it can cause long-term health problems.[6] The more ACEs a child experiences, the more likely they will experience toxic stress.

Exposure to ACEs can cause a range of issues for the child now and in the future. Potentially, ACEs can:

- Lower the stress threshold. This can result in non-attentive behaviours, aggression or defiance.
- Cause difficulty with learning and memory.
- Lead to learning and working memory problems in school and increase the probability of low educational attainment.
- Increase the difficulty of making friends and establishing/maintaining relationships with others.
- Damage the immune system due to the activation of stress hormones on a frequent or long-term basis. This can affect the body's ability to fight infection.
- Increase the heart rate, blood pressure, breathing and muscle tension due to exposure to toxic stress. The child will focus on the fight or flight response with the result that the thinking brain is not activated. This may lead to lasting health problems.[7]

ACEs are usually placed into three categories:[8]

1. Abuse

This is physical, mental and/or sexual abuse.

2. Neglect

Both physical and emotional neglect are included in this category.

3. Household Dysfunction

This can include a range of experiences, including having a relative with a mental illness, divorce/separation, experiencing or observing domestic violence, having a relative incarcerated in detention or prison, and substance-abuse or addiction issues.

However, additional ACEs have been suggested:

- Bullying/violence of/by another child, sibling or adult;
- Homelessness and/or substandard housing;
- Involvement in the child-welfare system;
- Medical trauma;
- Natural disasters (including climate change) and war;
- Racism, sexism or any other form of discrimination;
- Intergenerational or historical trauma;
- Poverty;
- Unemployment;
- Violence in the community.[9]

The ACEs Study

The ACEs Study published in 1998 is a significant study into the link between childhood adversity and ongoing health and wellbeing issues.[10]

In the 1980s, Dr. Vince Felitti worked for the Kaiser Permanente Health Appraisal Clinic in San Diego. He became interested in investigating why there was such a high dropout rate and subsequent weight gain for those enrolled in their obesity programs. He had thought there might be a link between childhood sexual abuse and obesity.

Dr. Felitti partnered with the Centres for Disease Control and Prevention (Dr. Robert Anda) to study the relationship between childhood experiences and future life outcomes. In the study, they interviewed over 17,000 people. They asked about health history and childhood experiences. In particular, they were interested in physical abuse, emotional abuse, sexual abuse, physical neglect, emotional neglect, domestic violence, substance abuse, parental separation/divorce and parental incarceration.

The study found that adverse childhood experiences were widespread. 2 out of 3 people reported one or more, and 1 out of

8 reported four or more of these adverse experiences. They also found that the more ACEs experienced, the greater the chance of health-related issues or substance abuse. Additionally, they found that those with a higher number of ACEs may also have a lower life expectancy.

Several studies have endorsed the findings of the original ACEs Study. They have found an increased risk of several potential health issues. For example, a 2016 study[11] by Ashton et al. on the Welsh population found increased risk of associated harms for people with four or more ACEs compared to those with no ACEs. The increased risks are summarised in the table below.

Potential Issue	Increased Likelihood (four or more ACEs vs. no ACEs)
Heart or respiratory disease or to have attended (or stayed overnight) in a hospital	3 times more likely
High risk drinker	4 times more likely
Received treatment for a Mental Illness	6 times more likely
Smoker	6 times more likely
have had or caused an unplanned teenage pregnancy	6 times more likely
Violent towards another in the past year	15 times more likely
Heroin/Crack use	16 times more likely
Incarcerated	20 times more likely

The participants in the original study were primarily middle class, white and with tertiary-level educational qualifications. This has led to some criticism about how relevant the study may be to those from other backgrounds. However, other studies have shown similar findings about the impact of adverse childhood experiences across various demographics.

ACEs also have potential impacts of increased chance of teen pregnancy, increased risk of contracting sexually transmitted diseases and increased risk of criminality and involvement in anti-social behaviour.

CHAPTER 3:

Healing

All is not lost. Our brains are incredible. They retain plasticity throughout our lives and can change. Our bodies can heal. Poor neural connections can be rewired and people can change their behaviour. The US Centers for Disease Control and Prevention has extrapolated that if we could reduce or prevent ACEs, the following reductions in health conditions, risky health behaviours and socioeconomic challenges could occur:[12]

Condition, Behaviour or Challenge	Potential Reduction
Depression	44%
Smoking	33%
Chronic Obstructive Pulmonary Disease (COPD)	27%
Heavy Alcohol Consumption	24%
Asthma	24%
Kidney Disease	16%
Stroke	15%
Heart Disease	13%
Cancer	6%
Diabetes	6%
Obesity	2%

It sounds pretty incredible, doesn't it? The potential is amazing. But how do we work to make this happen?

How Do We Reduce or Prevent ACEs?

There is so much we can do to reduce and prevent ACEs. Just as the positive support of a caring adult can buffer a child going through a stressful experience, positive life experiences can assist in buffering against these negative life experiences. Some of these positive life experiences include:

- Strong social relationships.
- Caregivers responding to their children. As mentioned in Chapter 1, this is sometimes called serve and return, a little like tennis. The child serves up an action and the caregiver returns with a response. This happens when a baby smiles and a parent returns the smile or a baby cries and the parent changes its nappy.
- Social supports.

One of the essential things we can do is work to build resilience in children. This can be done by providing the child with a safe environment and modelling resilient behaviour. This can include problem-solving actions and displaying healthy relationships with other people. Parents who build strong and nurturing relationships with their children are already building resilience. By listening and responding in a patient manner, the child receives support. At the same time, listening to their concerns and needs builds attachment and helps build further resilience.

Taking care of the child's physical needs will assist in building resilience. Providing a child with safe housing, nutritious and healthy food, necessary healthcare, ensuring they get appropriate sleep and rest when required, and giving them the opportunity to play all contribute to this resilience.

It is important to remember none of us are born parents. We often learn through how our parents parented us, and they learnt from their parents and others they observed. Often, we need to relearn much of what we have taken for granted as parenting, as some parenting techniques are counterproductive. One of the things parents can do is to learn about other parenting styles and gain knowledge on how children develop. This can help to become a more capable parent and become aware of what will likely happen as children grow.

One of the problematic areas can be assisting children to interact healthily with others, regulate and manage emotions, express their feelings, and rebound after loss and pain.[13] These are hard lessons to learn, but sometimes a hug goes a long way.

Following is a brief list of potential interventions that may be used to counter, reduce and prevent ACEs:

- **Social connection.** This is one of the most essential things that can be done to treat trauma. We, as humans, are social beings. Traumatic events can isolate us. Building social connections with others and finding our community is one of the greatest things we can do to reduce the impact of adverse experiences and heal from trauma.
- **Early intervention for families.** In a perfect world, parents would be supported with medical interventions and other supports from conception through to birth and after birth. This would include regular nurse visits, prenatal classes, parent support groups, parenting classes and programs, anger management programs and mindfulness training. None of us are born as great parents, but we can all learn how to be better and more supportive parents.
- **Strengthening economic support for families.** This could include, for example, family friendly work policies,

assistance with childcare costs, and parental leave. Raising a child can be a costly experience. Many people are impacted financially, with some living in poverty. Families can be caught in a poverty trap without economic support and feel there is no way out. This only adds to the stress and deepens the trauma being experienced. While we have a social and political policy setting where we accept poverty as the norm, we will continue to have people impacted by trauma and associated ACEs.

- **Promoting social norms that protect against violence and adversity**. For example, this could include public education campaigns about violence, legislation, parenting programs, and encouraging people to speak up when they see violence and abuse.
- **Teaching skills and strategies to handle stress, manage emotions and everyday challenges.**
- **Early childhood home visitation by health and other practitioners.**
- **Childcare and affordable early childhood education.**
- **Mentoring programs**. The availability and presence of an adult, external to the family, can be critical in helping young people navigate the changes that come with puberty and make the transition from teenager to adult.
- **After-school programs**. These allow the parent to continue making an income while providing the child with a safe learning and play environment
- **Raising awareness of ACEs and shifting the focus from individual responsibility to community solutions.** Too often, we blame the victim or simply dismiss ACEs and their impact as "bad parenting", whereas we need to work from a position of empathy and understand the impact that ACEs can have on a person.

Trauma Can Occur at Any Time

We have focused on adverse childhood experiences (ACEs). However, trauma can occur at any time. We can all experience traumatic events as adults not related to childhood trauma. It is important to remember that any trauma can change our brain architecture and can activate our stress response, resulting in us being in a state of hypervigilance. Many of us know those who have returned from military service who may be moody, jittery at certain sounds, angry and depressed.

We accept they may have post-traumatic stress disorder and require support to recover. This disorder developed through their traumatic experiences and what they had witnessed occurring to others in a war zone. But other events can be traumatising, such as an accident, a natural disaster or a violent action. These can result in trauma, and post-traumatic stress disorder could develop for anyone experiencing these events.

We can reduce ACEs and their impact, but we also have the opportunity to support and buffer others who have had a traumatic experience that has impacted their wellbeing.

A Trauma-Informed Approach

In examining trauma and meeting with people who may have experienced it, a trauma- informed or aware approach is the only viable approach. This approach begins with the knowledge that trauma is a widespread experience and can impact people in many ways. "Trauma-informed practices aren't judgemental (e.g., he/she/they are "good" or "bad" neighbours) and instead understand that all human beings need to feel safe and be heard for them to make any significant personal changes."[14] In this approach, the person is at the centre. Their wellbeing is central to the aim of doing no harm to the person. The question asked is not what is wrong with the person but what has happened to the person. Taking this approach, we stop seeing the person as a sum of their problems or through the lens of their behaviour. However, their current behaviour is a result of their cumulative life experiences and relationships with others. An aggressive behavioural response may be their only way to deal with authority or a stressful situation. It is a symptom of their trauma.

Positive relationships with others and positive experiences are the path to healing. "When you have friends, family, and other healthy people in your life, you have a natural healing environment. We heal best in community."[15]

Who Should Use a Trauma-Informed Approach?

If a trauma-informed approach values and sees the person, then who should use a trauma-informed approach? Should it only be those specialist practitioners, such as case workers, who work with people who have experienced trauma in their lives? Or can a trauma-informed approach be relevant in broader and other contexts?

A trauma-informed approach is non-judgemental and seeks to make the person feel safe. It is aimed at pursuing the wellbeing of the individual while doing no harm. It can apply to anyone who meets with people. It should not be restricted to specialist workers, social workers, psychologists and child- protection workers but to almost everyone interacting with people during their day. This applies equally to those who work in hospitality, retail, reception and administration as it applies to any community-sector professional. This is because all these groups of people will come across others who have suffered severe trauma and still carry the wound.

I consider that any clever business operator or senior manager would see the potential of treating people with dignity and respect and seeing past the behaviours triggered by their trauma.

Let's look further at how trauma can be healed.

Positive and Adverse Childhood Experiences (PACEs)

We've already been discussing the idea of positive childhood experiences (PCEs) in countering and preventing ACEs. Some positive experiences can be part of the healing process. This is the exciting part about our amazing brains. We've already briefly mentioned that our brains keep changing. This continues throughout life but is most active in the early years of life and again at puberty. But it continues to change throughout our life at a slower rate. Just as adverse experiences change how our brains are wired, so do positive experiences.

Our brain is continually changing. Every interaction we have, every experience and every sensory interaction with the environment changes our brain. Most of the time, we don't even recognise it is happening. Just as toxic stress changes the architecture and wiring of our brain, so does the removal of this stress and replacing it with positive practices that build resilience. The brain can slowly undo many of the stress-induced changes.

There is a growing body of research showing the impact of positive experiences countering the impact of ACEs on a person's life and wellbeing.[16] The excellent news is that the research on ACEs and the growing body of research on PACEs is being used to provide better outcomes for people. Examples of this are easy to see happening around us. They may include the local doctor who screens patients for their childhood experiences and designs interventions accordingly. This may mean referral to other supports instead of a purely chemical-based intervention. Or organisations becoming informed on how trauma impacts people and how they can better respond to people based on this information. It includes training people on the impact of ACEs on their lives and how positive actions can start the healing process. There are also examples of the use of research in ACEs and PACEs in responding to youth crime, suicide and teen pregnancy.[17]

Those who take this approach are taking what has been referred to as a "trauma-informed approach". It refers to how an organisation or community thinks about and responds to children and adults who have experienced or may be at risk of experiencing trauma. In this approach, the whole community understands the prevalence and impact of ACEs, the role trauma plays in people's lives, and the complex and varied paths for healing and recovery.

A trauma-informed approach asks: "What happened to you?" instead of "What's wrong with you?" It is designed to avoid re-traumatising already traumatised people, with a focus on "safety first" (including emotional safety) and a commitment to do no harm. However, a trauma-informed approach is most successful when an organisation or community builds policies and practices based on a foundation of science and research into ACEs and other trauma.[18]

Our Healing Place

For each of us, there is a place where healing occurs. It is a place where we find others. Those with similar interests and mindsets or those with whom we have something in common. This is our healing place. It is our community.

CHAPTER 4:

Community

O ne thing common in much of the research on preventing and healing trauma is the importance of social connection: community.

The research on trauma shows that those who have experienced some degree of healing have a greater sense of wellbeing, lower rates of mental health illness, are less isolated and lonely, have a greater chance of longevity, feel less fear and apprehension about their safety and are in more positive relationships with others compared to those with untreated trauma.

At the same time, the research on connected communities shows that those who live their lives in connection with others exhibit precisely the same potential as those who have experienced little trauma or who have had the experience of healing from their trauma.

The common key to both is social connection. We are social beings. We are "hardwired" to be in relationships with each other. We are not meant to live in isolation. We crave social contact and this is where our greatest healing occurs. "We are a social species; we are meant to be in community—emotionally, socially, and physically interconnected with others. Look at the fundamental organisation and functioning of the human body, including the brain. You will see that so much of it is intended to help us create, maintain, and manage social interactions. We are relational creatures."[19]

Community: What is it?

So, what do we mean by the term community?

Community is one of those "catch all" words and can be used in several contexts. It can mean different things to different people. In its most straightforward sense, community can be described as the result of those things we share in common. It is the experience of what we share together that creates community. This commonality of sharing can mean different things to each person, and all of us may experience different types of community on a daily basis.

Government authorities will often speak of community in a macro setting. For example, the Australian community. This usage drags diverse groups and individuals into one collective, with the one aspect they share in common being the country where they live.

Then, there are communities of interest where people share a common concern or feature. This is where we have the sporting community, arts community or the community that springs up around an issue such as an environmental problem or the disability community.

We can also have the community of those we work with, our colleagues. Our shared interest is our work and the place where our work is conducted.

Then, we can label our online connections as a community. Although there is no physical contact or face-to-face communication, online platforms allow people with shared concerns or interests to meet and interact.

So, what are the common threads in all of these communities? Community involves the development of interpersonal relationships based on something we share in common with each other and the commitments we make with each other and ourselves to act on this shared interest or concern. This draws us together to create that social phenomenon we call community.[20]

We are drawn together over something we share in common. Once drawn together, we begin to build relationships with each other and become concerned about each other's wellbeing. It is in relationships like this that we heal.

In the context of healing trauma, the type of community I am most interested in is the community of locality (i.e., where we live and work). This community is based on place. It is the community of our daily experience. This is not to say that other community experiences will not aid in our healing, as social connection is the key. But the community of place is where we can meet each other face-to-face. It's where we meet our physical, emotional, social, psychological and spiritual needs most easily. Online communities and other communities of interest do play a significant role in healing. However, the daily experience of building relationships with others as we go about our day is where the ongoing healing experience occurs.

There is the temptation to speak of some mythological past community. We all know this type of concept of community. The one where a neighbour calls around for a "cup of sugar". I'm not sure this type of community has ever existed except in our imaginations and media reimagining the "good old days". We are also not talking about the community of our memories. For me, that would be the community where dad went to work and mum stayed home. After school, we would play in the street with our neighbourhood friends until the sun set and it was time to return home for dinner.

This was a community of a different time and one that may be enhanced over time by my memory.

Instead, we are talking about what we mean by community in the contemporary sense (i.e., how and where we live now). This will mean creating a sense of community beginning with the people we live with, then our neighbours, then others in our street, suburb and town/city. For some, this will include their work community, online communities and social media. But the most immediate community is that community where we live.

In many ways, most of our communities are very different to what they were in the past. Both men and women now work, and often more than one job to simply "make ends meet". Our houses are usually empty during the day. Children go to school and then to after-school care. Once home, there is little opportunity for children to play with others from the neighbourhood; if this happened, it would rarely be outside in the street. Often, there is television or other devices. Most of us don't know our neighbours and most of us spend next to no time in our front yards with the result that we don't even see our neighbours. In 2018, *The Australian Loneliness Survey* found that 70% of Australians would have no neighbour they could talk to about important matters; 40% see their neighbours less than once a month; and 47% have no neighbours they could call on if they needed help.[21] This is a much different world from the reimagined community of my childhood.

Over the course of two generations, our society and communities have changed rapidly. We have moved from a place where we knew our neighbours to often isolated existences. In the past, the common good was highly valued. Our communities are now centred on consumerism and the individual. They are places where the needs and desires of the individual are central, above the needs and desires of the rest of the community. There are consequences to these social changes. More people are living lonely, isolated lives. We now have fewer friends than we have had in the past, and we rarely invite people into our homes for a meal or a party. We no longer welcome the stranger. The rise of the individual has come at the cost of the value of the whole.

To counter this social change, we are driven to consider what community means for us here and now and what it means to be part of a community. The "we instead of me". This reverses how we see not only ourselves but also our society. When the focus is on the individual we often fail to address underlying social issues. The focus also shifts from what can be achieved through harnessing the power of community and what can be done for the common good. This results in short-term solutions. Immediate solutions are sought. We stop seeing our role as community members of creating change and relegate this responsibility to others. To government. The only possible outcome is that things are done to us, not by us. We begin operating in a deficit mode where we only look at what needs to be fixed. Doctors, therapists and service providers ask us what is wrong with us. Services operate to "fix" perceived problems and fulfil perceived needs. The more we are asked questions about what is wrong with us, the easier it is to see that we are the problem and we begin seeing ourselves and our communities as being in deficit. The riches found in every community are overlooked and lost. Members of these communities shoulder the blame for social and economic problems outside of their control. No one chooses to live in poverty; it results from the political, social and economic systems operating at the time. The skills we all have, our own personal strengths and the gifts our communities offer are ignored.

However, the reverse is where the truth lies. We are not a drag on the resources of our society. It is not the individual's fault that the situation is not conducive to their wellbeing. The scars of traumatic events are not our fault. They were inflicted on us. They are what happened to us, not who we are. When we come together, we find many others in the same situation. You are not alone. The problem is not us. It is not our fault; instead, we can understand that we have a shared social problem requiring shared attention. It is a problem that needs not just to rest on the shoulders of one person but is a problem for all of us to bear.[22]

To find our community, those who share what we have in common with us, will take deliberate action. It involves reaching out to others. In doing this, we find we are not alone. Others share the same problems and we all have gifts, talents, skills and assets to share in not only working to be healed but also to solve critical social problems. We can use our assets and gifts to create a stronger and more agile community. A healing community.

The healthy, connected community is where we grow and where we heal. This is our healing place. Social connection is central to healing trauma. This is where we find our place of rest and the support to recover and move forward. "Your connected-ness to other people is so key to buffering any current stressor— and to healing from past trauma. Being with people who are present, supportive, and nurturing. Belonging."[23]

One of the reasons why community is our healing place and relationships are central to our healing is that when we are in safe, loving and caring relationships with others, this allows us to revisit our trauma in doses that we can deal with and still be safe and protected. "Creating a network—a village, whatever you want to call it—gives you opportunities to revisit trauma in moderate, controllable doses. That pattern of stress activation will ultimately lead to a more regulated stress-reactivity Curve."[24]

CHAPTER 5:

A Healthy Community?

In Chapter 4, we discussed the importance of forming social connections with others and building a community where we can build relationships with our neighbours. In this chapter, we will continue to explore the foundations of healing together. We will briefly examine four functions of a healthy community that build a firm base for healing from trauma.

The Functions of a Healthy, Connected Community

A connected community has several positive outcomes for all and is our place of healing. Cormac Russell and John McKnight in their 2022 book *The Connected Community*[25] have recognised and highlighted seven main interrelated functions of a connected community. These functions are common to any community with strong connections between its members:

1. Enabling health;
2. Ensuring security;
3. Stewarding ecology;
4. Shaping local economies;
5. Contributing to local food production;
6. Raising our children;
7. Co-creating care.[26]

Although all seven functions are important and hallmarks of a connected community, our discussion of healing from trauma will be restricted to four that are probably the most relevant to healing. We will briefly discuss enabling health, ensuring security, raising our children, and co-creating care.

Enabling Health

It might come as a surprise but doctors, hospitals and medicine are not the primary sources of our health and wellbeing. In reality, the community is the primary source of our health. Certainly, the medical fraternity has some real importance in helping us maintain our health and support when medical assistance is required, but it is social connection that provides us with the most important health benefits.

Being connected to those around us provides us with the optimum environment to live a healthy and full life. In particular, those who live in a connected and strong community receive the following benefits:

- 50% chance of increased longevity;
- Increased immunity;
- Decreased rates of anxiety and depression;
- Increased self-esteem and empathy;
- Regulation of emotions;
- Social connection that creates a feedback loop of social, emotional and physical wellbeing;
- A quicker recovery from disaster.[27]

However, if you are not connected socially with others, then your health and wellbeing can deteriorate. In our modern world people are increasingly disconnected from others. Loneliness and feelings of isolation are increasing. This growing social problem has been recognised in Great Britain where they have established a government ministry responsible for loneliness and isolation. Our sense of social connection is decreasing. Although it is possible to have 100 friends on social media, the quality of these connections is in question. Are they real connections, friends who will be there when we need the support or are they friends in name only? The result is that while we can spend a large amount of time on social media and attract a high number of "friends", we can still be isolated and cut off from those around us.

The solution seems reasonably straightforward. We are not beings meant to live in isolation. We are interdependent on each other and need to be in relationships with each other. Being in a relationship with others has substantial health benefits. We need to make real connections with those around us. With family, neighbours, work colleagues and others we are fortunate enough to meet. While social media can provide some support, it is those we meet in our daily lives who can provide the most important and substantial support.

Ensuring Security

One of our basic human needs is feeling safe. When we don't feel safe, our limbic system is activated and stress hormones are released to prepare us to fight or run. As we've seen, this can result in toxic stress and places us at risk of becoming traumatised. However, if we live in a connected community, we will have a real sense of safety and where we live will be a safe place. A safe community is a place where people feel safe both day and night. People feel secure enough to go for a walk by themselves, they don't see every stranger as a potential criminal, and the thought that they could become a victim of crime is not even a consideration.

Many security contractors recognise that spending time getting to know your neighbours is one of the simplest and most important things a person can do to improve the safety of the street and suburb where they live. Often this is viewed through the lens of increasing passive surveillance (i.e., if people know their neighbours, they develop a level of trust and concern for each other). They are therefore more likely to be more aware if something is out of place in the neighbourhood or if something not quite right is occurring. From a crime-prevention position, getting to know our neighbours sets a social process in motion. When people get to know each other, they begin to build a relationship. Every relationship is governed by rules called norms. These are behavioural expectations around others and in the places where people meet. Some behaviours are viewed as acceptable and proper by the majority of people in that place, while other behaviours are seen as unacceptable and inappropriate. A norm of behaviour is established and there are sanctions for not following this norm. Unacceptable behaviours will not be tolerated. The more neighbours we know by name, the more people subscribe to the same norm and behavioural expectations, and the safer our neighbourhood becomes.

We have the power to create a safe place where we live. While creating safe places is frequently seen as a responsibility of the state through the provision of a police service or something contracted to private security services, this is not a proactive strategy and does not create a safe place. The role of the police is to enforce written law and act after an incident that has breached the law. Or with security services, their role is to monitor a situation and report any breaches of the law to the police. However, as community members, we are not bound by reactive strategies and acting only after an event has occurred. We have the power at our fingertips to create a safe and welcoming environment in our streets and reduce the likelihood of a crime being committed. We have already discussed how getting to know our neighbours creates the environment for a street, neighbourhood or community to be seen as a safe place.

Another factor in creating a safe place is how frequently we use the space in our neighbourhood. This will include not only the usage of parks, playgrounds and walking tracks but also how often we are in the front yard and driveway of our houses. The more present we are in those spaces being viewed by our neighbours and those passing by, the safer an area becomes. And when people feel safe in the street where they live they are more likely to spend more time outside their home exercising, gardening, walking the dog, etc. As far as crime prevention is concerned, this creates more opportunities for surveillance. A person contemplating a crime is unlikely to act on this urge if there is a chance they will be observed, reported to the police and caught. If you feel safe in your house and your street, then you live in a safe area. Just keep spending time outside and enjoy where you live.

The two important components of creating a safe place are:

1. The number of neighbours we know by their first name.
2. How often we are outside our house and present in the street.[28]

Several community-centred approaches can also have a major impact on safety in our neighbourhoods. These include mentoring youth, restorative justice and alternative sentencing approaches such as circle sentencing. These have the potential to be highly successful as they treat both the victim and alleged perpetrator with dignity and allow the perpetrator to take responsibility and be accountable for their actions. We will look at some of these actions in detail in Chapter 9.

Raising Our Children

"It takes a village to raise a child." How easily these words roll off of our lips. We know this is true but have we forgotten how to create this village? The problem is that it is no longer the village that raises our children. We have corporatised the raising of our children and contracted it out away from the village. Child care is now a career path. And it is provided in childcare centres. It is no longer provided by the village in our homes and our streets. However, we still need the village to raise the child. We need the support of those around us to raise our children. The village is still central to raising our children. But it is only possible when we live in a community where we have a relational connection with others in our neighbourhood.

In a connected community, the village has the potential to provide:

- An important relationship environment. Children will copy the actions and behaviours they see in the home and the village that surrounds them. This provides an opportunity for acceptable and appropriate behaviours and relationships to be modelled. "A child's relationship environment begins in the family, but then extends to adults and peers outside of the family who have important roles in their life."[29]
- Belonging, a sense of identity and learning opportunities. Once we connect with others in our neighbourhood, we start to feel a connection. This in turn promotes a connection to place, to the area we live in. It is the same with children. A sense of belonging to family, to place, to the village is important in a child developing their identity and feeling safe. "Children's understanding of their self is developed through relationships and in the context of their families and communities."[30]

44

- Support for active participation in the world and continuity of learning.
- Supportive relationships and resource networks to connect children and families.

We need to be in a connected community to find and build the village for our children to grow and develop fully. Isolated from the village, this cannot happen.

Co-Creating Care

Cormac Russell and John McKnight have provided a wonderful term to describe how we are all involved in caring for one another in "co-creating care".[31] We create an environment of care together. Community can be the site of care. This is especially so when we get to know our neighbours. We build trust between them and us, and "social capital" grows. With the development of trust comes a desire to care for others. We start to look out for our neighbours and become concerned about their wellbeing.

As neighbours, we begin to care for each other. We start to notice when things change in our street. We become concerned if we haven't seen one of our neighbours for a few days. We start to feel safe with our neighbours and can trust them to care for our children when needed. If we have a connection with our neighbours, we trust them enough to care for our children if we need to go on an errand quickly. And we trust they would feel the same level of safety with their children in our care.

We often think that institutions (organisations, services and early learning facilities) provide care. This is not exactly correct. These places are a source of service, not care. They are services where their employees are paid to care. Even though they may be dedicated and have a passion for their community, it is doubtful they would be in a caring role if they weren't adequately reimbursed. They are not care providers but providers of a service.

In summary, care is central to being in community.

The connections and relationships we create build community. When we join together with each other, we show our care for children, neighbours and the place where we live. This provides ongoing opportunities for healing from trauma.

CHAPTER 6:

Design and the Healing Community

In Chapter 5, we mentioned very briefly the role of design in creating a safe place. In this chapter, we will explore in a little more detail the role of how our streets, suburbs, towns and cities are designed to facilitate and support the healing community.

The Role of Urban Design in Creating Community

How we design our cities, towns, villages and suburbs has an impact on how we connect as a community. We can design streets for cars or we can design streets for people. We can design houses so that they invite a community lifestyle or we can design our homes so that they shut us off from others in our neighbourhood. We can design streetscapes that discourage criminal and anti-social behaviour or we can create urban settings that encourage this type of unwanted behaviour. A community-ty-friendly streetscape is a safer streetscape as it provides opportunities for people to linger. This encourages social interaction and connection. A community of connected people is a safer place to be.

Urban design that encourages high motor vehicle usage is not a design approach that encourages community connection. These types of designs convey an impression that an area is a place to drive through, not a place to slow down and experience. When there is an emphasis on cars over people, the first casualty is a sense of safety. Streets with a design focus on getting from point A to point B are streets that often need to be retrofitted to slow traffic down to a safer pace. When retrofitting occurs, it involves traffic-calming measures such as electronic speed indicator signage, speed warning signs, traffic islands for pedestrian safety and traffic lights. These are the places where residents may feel the need to erect signage in their front yards enforcing a message for drivers to slow down. They are not streets where parents and children feel safe walking or riding bikes and scooters.

They are also not streets where children can play. They are not safe places to kick a ball or play games in. This sense of a lack of safety is even worse because many of these streets lack basic pedestrian infrastructure such as walkways and footpaths. The result is that access for people with physical disabilities, sensory impairments or parents with young children is reduced. They are often forced onto the side of the road, placing them at greater risk of coming into contact with motor vehicles.

Opposed to this is the urban landscape that invites people to walk or ride bicycles and use the street for community-friendly activities. These types of streetscapes feature low vehicular access or traffic is designed to move at a slower pace, and footpaths form a connecting network to make it a simple process for pedestrians to get from one place to another in safety. People are encouraged to linger and talk to others they meet. People exercise by jogging and exploring different pedestrian options, and parents are observed walking with prams and strollers. People walk their dogs. As well as the inclusion of footpaths, other pedestrian-friendly items may be included such as walking tracks and safe cycleways to encourage people to explore the local area.

To use a buzz term, these are "liveable places".

Houses are designed so they face the street and their front doors are readily observable from the street. Houses are set back to encourage the usage of front yards and high fences are discouraged. This all increases passive surveillance which reduces the opportunity for crime to be committed. The increased communication between neighbours that this type of people-friendly design encourages has the bonus of reducing loneliness and isolation and creating a greater sense of wellbeing in the area.

Opposed to this is design that encourages more time inside the house, restricting incidental contact between neighbours. People reduce efforts to communicate with their neighbours, depleting stocks of social capital and increasing their suspicion of others. The stranger is no longer welcome. The eventual result is a reduction in feelings of safety. Fear increases. Fence heights are increased, home security is beefed up and social media posts reflect a perception of the fear of crime with the inevitable result of an increase in social disconnection.

Unfortunately, design discouraging a communal lifestyle often wins. But it doesn't have to be this way. So often, it seems as though we have forgotten the power a community has when we work together to create change. Nothing is changed if we wait for the government to initiate change. Things only change when we work together to force or convince those who hold the formal power to make the changes we want to see happen in our communities. Of course, change more readily happens if there is access to valuable others within the government who hold political sway or other power bases.

The Role of Local Government

Local government is the level of government closest to the community. Elected representatives (councillors) will come from the local community. People working for local government will often come from the community they serve. They are often community members with a stake in what happens to their community. Often there will be a councillor or council staff member who will provide a listening ear to what the community has to say and will respond with some type of action. They are important assets in building stronger communities.

It is easy to forget that the language we use and allow others to use is important. Language conveys our message and is critical in creating our reality. When confronting situations where a change in policy or local government approach is needed or beneficial, the language we choose to use in the discussion is even more important. It will convey to the recipient not just what we want or why but also an image of the reality we wish to create through the requested change.

Contemporary governments view themselves as being part of the corporate world. They operate from the business model of the corporation. It is not uncommon for mayors of local councils to describe the organisation in terms of a multi-million-dollar-a-year business. However, this is a flawed way to view government and how it operates. It ignores the core value of local government in serving and maintaining the community. Ideally, one of our aims is to use language reflecting the purpose of local government: to serve the people.

The language used about the community is central to our discussion. We are not customers, consumers, clients or participants. We are community members, residents, ratepayers and citizens. Government is not a business or selling a product, but an agent of service to the community. It exists to support and maintain the wellbeing of the community. Without the community, it cannot exist. This perspective turns the power imbalance on its head. I recently heard a story of a council manager who expressed the current role of many local government bodies as "We are up here and you are down there."

In other words, the manager saw that local government makes the decisions and organisations, services and community members are on the receiving end with no participation or power in the equation. I have also observed situations where the local council disbanded its community committees. These are committees of residents who have provided councils with valuable information about how residents view particular issues and council actions, and they often provide advice on potential ways that the council can move forward with addressing various matters. There may be reasons for disbanding these committees, such as replacing them with a broader consultative process. But in those situations where a replacement process was not initiated, I propose the main reason is that the council representatives attending the meetings didn't like what they were hearing from the committee or found it challenging.

The aim is to turn this approach on its head with the community informing the council on how local government can best serve the community. The power we hold as a community and as citizens is to demand that our local government lives up to this expectation and returns to being a servant of the community. After all, there is a reason why government employees were once called public servants. We can work with our local government to ensure their actions are in the best interests of the whole community. That urban design is for people and works to make building strong, connected communities a reality. We can work with the government to develop an understanding that the creation of physical infrastructure such as streets, roads and urban subdivisions is not only enhanced by the building of community, but that the concrete structure is worthless unless the community is central to its design. It is not just the role of community development staff employed by the council to be involved in community building, it is the role of all who serve in local government either as elected representatives or employees.

Additionally, community members can form partnerships with the local government to assist in maintaining the assets of the community. Members of the community possess a powerful tool in voluntary labour to assist their local government authority in maintaining local assets. For example, many councils have park care groups of community members where the council lacks the resources to adequately perform park care services. Or there may be similar groups to encourage community involvement in the care of assets. My local council has responsibility for many walking tracks and natural areas. They have a large program incorporating the labour of community members to maintain these walking tracks and care for the green space. Without this essential work, these spaces would quickly deteriorate. Council depends on this labour. We already often have these partnerships and are already in a positive working relationship with the council.

Perhaps these relationships could be useful in leveraging better urban design and a focus on building the local community. In achieving this change in how local government operates, some questions should remain front and centre in our deliberations:

1. **What can we do for ourselves?** A consumer/client model of service provision and government intervention is one where members of the community are seen as being inadequate to do things for themselves. Change can only come from services provided by an outside service or government. The problem is there are many things that communities can do for themselves but they have been convinced that nothing can happen without the assistance and guidance of those in authority. In

reality, communities need to uncover their local assets, and mobilise and connect those assets to create change. When faced with an issue or a challenging situation, the community could first ask itself if there is something that can be done using its own resources.

2. **What do we need some assistance with?** There are times when external assistance is valuable. Sometimes all the assets are not located in one place or external professional advice may be needed or some short-term funding may be required to assist in making change a reality. And there are times when working in partnership can create change quicker and more successfully. Often councils will be more than willing to lend their expertise for a project where the community provides the labour. This can be an attractive option as it is often a lower-cost proposal for the successful implementation of the project. For example, if a community had volunteer labour to install a footpath but lacked the design, engineering expertise or physical resources for the project, the local council may provide the missing elements and partner with the volunteers to install the footpath. Again, it should be a decision of the community as to when and who they reach out to for assistance.

3. **What can we not complete on our own and needs to be handed over to someone else?** There are always those times when the community itself cannot achieve the necessary change. These are times when it is up to an external body, group, agency or government authority to be in control to complete a necessary action. For example, policing is not a role a community should undertake. This should always be in the hands of the police and the criminal justice system.

4. **What are the things that others need to stop doing?** Of course, there will be situations where another external agency will need to be told that an intervention is not required or even part of their brief. This is particularly so when communities have accepted it to be the role of government to do everything for them. There will be times when the government will need to be told to stop what they are doing and leave it to someone else, such as the community, to undertake.

5. **Are there things the government should be doing that they are not currently undertaking?** There will always be situations where an action is part of the brief of an agency, organisation or government and where they will need to be told that action is required. For example, local government is well-positioned to be involved in community development work. However, with a move from a community focus to a corporate focus, this work is easily portrayed as being outside the scope of local government when in reality the creation of a community is the core function of any government.

These are the questions that a connected, motivated and strong community will ask. Although the preferred option is for the community to take the lead on creating change, there will be times when this is not possible and partnerships will need to be made or other organisations asked to take the required action.

The 15-Minute City

I grew up in a regional centre. Although small in international terms at 25,000 people, it was the regional centre for agricultural products, and housed the region's largest hospital and regional mental healthcare facilities. It had an abattoir to process meat products and other manufacturing industries. At the time it also had a tertiary institution, so there was a lower need for young people to move out of the region to further their education. The town housed many government services including a prison for the state's most hardened criminals. It was also the centre for a number of regional government services. In many ways, it was a self-contained city that met the needs of its residents.

This was a time before the existence of large shopping malls and before the supply of food was dominated by two or three supermarket chains. For shopping needs in between the large weekly shopping excursions into the main street of the city, there were corner or general stores. These local businesses provided the staples such as bread, milk and some fruit and vegetables, as well as lollies and soft drinks to tempt the children. Three of these businesses were an easy walking distance from my home. As children, we knew the name of the local shopkeeper and they knew our names and the names of our parents. If we misbehaved in the shop, our parents would hear about it often before we arrived home. Across the road from one of these corner stores was the local butchery where our weekly meat supplies would be purchased. Again, the butcher and his staff knew our names and our parents.

My father was self-employed and ran his business from home as a semi-skilled labourer. Even if people had to work away from home, it was only within a ten-to-fifteen-minute walk or bike ride away from their homes.

All of this helped build a connected and supportive community.

Now almost all of these old corner stores are gone. Driven out of business by larger shopping centres where everything a person wanted to buy can be found under one roof. They also struggled against the competition and lower prices afforded by large grocery chains. They became unprofitable businesses. Their demise was a real loss to the establishment and growth of a strong community.

They provided places of information exchange, passive surveillance of what was happening in the neighbourhood, and a place where people would meet with each other as they shopped for items. Jim Diers has referred to these places as "bumping places".[32] This is a good term to describe them and their function. They provided an opportunity for people to bump into one another, deepen their relationships and grow the social capital between them.

One interesting contemporary urban design approach is finding some traction in this space—the 15-minute city. Proposed by Carlos Moreno, the concept is very simple. All that we need should be found within a 15-minute walk or ride from where we live. This should include housing, employment, shopping, entertainment and recreation. This approach "...puts people and their environment at the centre of urban planning... key elements are: the proximity of necessities; local participation and decision-making; community solidarity and connection; and green and sustainable urban living."[33] The 15-minute city represents a return to earlier times of town or village life to recreate the village. It's an attractive proposal. In smaller centres such as a country town, this is not such a major change to planning but in larger cities, it represents a real change in planning and design.

These are places where some workers make lengthy commutes from their homes to the CBD where they work. Even for these workers to conduct basic shopping for food and other groceries may mean a drive to another suburb where they have very little in common with other shoppers and business operators.

The 15-minute city has been viewed as a positive way for cities to recover from the impacts of the COVID-19 pandemic, to reduce the reliance on cars which in turn has an impact on the environment, and to improve mental health and wellbeing.[34] It is one planning method to aid in the building of community. It has the potential to provide those informal opportunities to heal from our trauma through interactions with other community members.

Some detractors of this urban planning theory have based their opposition on their experience of the COVID-19 pandemic where some suburbs and localities were in long-term lockdown enforced by governments. They fear that governments will use the 15-minute city as a tool to restrict their movements. This is an assumption that has no real relationship to the 15-minute city goal of making community, working and home life easier for all of us. It aims to lower the stresses of daily life and increase connected community. Any attempt to impose hard, regulated restrictions on the movement of people between localities and suburbs is certainly not in the spirit of the 15-minute city. Such an action would be strongly opposed by its proponents.

CHAPTER 7:

The Healing Community in Action

We've had some discussion about the role of the healing community and how it can not only be an important component in healing from trauma but also in creating safety, raising children and caring for others. In this chapter, we will look at the healing community in action.

Where are the Leaders?

Leadership in our communities is a real issue. Where are the leaders and who are the leaders?

How many times do we find that those leaders installed by government and other authorities are not fit for the task or those who put themselves forward as leaders fail so dismally?

The problem with community leadership is the same problem we face in managerial leadership. We tend to put leaders or managers on some type of pedestal. The expectation is that they will lead us out of the situation we are currently in. We seem to anticipate that they will somehow heroically rescue us. The problem here is that those who step forward or are selected are often not the right people to provide leadership. Our accepted model of leadership is one where the leader takes the lead from the front as if a community was some type of military campaign. This often only feeds the ego of the leader and achieves nothing for the community. Instead of a focus on who the leader is, we need to change the focus to the value or result of a particular course of action for the community. And then decide who is best placed to provide leadership for this result to be achieved. Another model is required to facilitate this change of focus.

One of the issues we have in seeking real leadership is to address our own expectations of who will take responsibility for creating the change we are looking for. So many times, when seeking to create change, address a problem or fix a local issue, the expectation is that someone else will do it. We have been conditioned to think this way over a number of generations. It is so easy to see it as someone else's responsibility. This is encouraged by government regulations of the things we are no longer permitted to do without explicit approval. It is further reinforced through the service-provision model we live with in our society. The result is that we are either looking for leaders outside of our community to do something and we become increasingly frustrated and feel even more powerless when nothing happens or changes. Or we look to our community leaders to make change a reality, often with the same result. We have all seen situations where those recognised as community leaders by government agencies and those locally elected or self-nominated leaders have failed their own communities.

However, there are alternate models of leadership.

One of these models comes from management theory. It is servant leadership. A servant leader is one who prepares their team, trains them and then steps back and lets them complete the task at hand. The leader is there to support them as required, providing a safety net. As one such leader has said: "I hire good people with the skills required for the job. I can't be with them as they do their job. I can only let them fulfil the role in the best way they can." This is leadership by standing back and is the style of leadership that provides a perfect model for community leadership.

There are several characteristics of this type of leadership. A servant leader is a good listener, empathetic, understands that the healing of others is central to the role, is self-aware, can persuade people without being forceful, maintains a vision of what can be achieved, prepares for the future (has foresight), operates as a steward (is accountable for their actions), is committed to the community and aims to build the community.[35]

The servant model of leadership is not a power-based model but one where those who are called to lead in a situation do so due to their own passions, gifts, skills or interests. They may only lead as the situation dictates and then step back once the situation has changed and others step up to lead. This is an ego-free style of leadership.

When we are discussing community change and community building, one of the qualities each one of us has is the ability, often unrecognised, to lead. This is a quality we all have and is part of who we are as humans. We are all born leaders. Often this is exhibited in those areas where our individual gifts, skills and passions are recognised and required for the situation at hand. We all have gifts to bring to the party. We are all leaders and can provide leadership when it is needed.

Unfortunately, this type of leadership is not readily recognised by outside institutions and services as it doesn't fit their leadership model, but it is the most essential form of leadership. It is not driven by ego but by service. It is very different from the generally accepted model of leadership. The leader enables other people to achieve great things by stepping back and allowing them to use their gifts. This leader sees their role as supporting others, removing barriers to them achieving and encouraging them to move forward. As Peter Block has written: "In communal transformation, leadership is about intention, convening, valuing relatedness and presenting choices. It is not a personality characteristic or a matter of style, and therefore it requires nothing more than what all of us already have."[36] With this broader model of leadership, we can all lead when the situation calls for us to offer our gifts, skills and other assets.

Although not recognised as leaders in other models, this servant-based approach recognises the role of those who have the gift of creating connection within communities. The person who has the ability and knowledge to connect people with common interests together, and the person who knows where someone can find that person who can show them how to learn a skill they desire to learn. These connecting people are in every street and often every family. They often don't put their hands up to take on a traditional leadership role. They may be part of a committee or organisation, but this is not their usual comfort zone. They are more comfortable at suggesting who might be better positioned to serve on the committee.

As Cormac Russell and John McKnight in *The Connected Community* have described these connectors: "They would be shocked to see themselves as leaders in the traditional sense of the word, where leaders are at the front of group galvanising followers around key issues. Connectors avoid the front of the crowd, and they are allergic to polarising issues because they are focused on authentic connections."[37]

These connectors know a high number of people in their local community. They are often involved in connecting people with each other. If you need to know how to learn a musical instrument, this is the person who will know who can teach you. They know their community and they know who to go to for assistance. These are the people we need to seek out when building our own local community. They are more likely to be serving tea and coffee rather than putting themselves forward as leaders. They serve and are aware of their community.

Although Russell and McKnight separate connectors from leadership roles due to leaders often being only interested in issues and solving problems,[38] I believe this servant-based model allows space for them to be viewed as leaders without seeing them as any more important than anyone else in the community. They have a role to play in building community and from time to time this will involve some degree of leadership, just as it will for all of us. What is required is changing our own mindset on how we view leadership. Better still, let's just change the title to servant.

Let's look at how this all works in practice. The following are examples and stories of the healing community in action where people actively provide servant leadership to create strong and connected local communities.

The Intentional Community

Intentional communities are those communities established for a specific purpose. The Foundation of Intentional Communities defines an intentional community as "a group of people who have chosen to live together or share resources on the basis of common values…Intentional communities model more cooperative, sustainable and just ways of life."[39]

This will include communities comprising those with similar interests and worldviews such as the alternative lifestyle communities or communes established in the late 1960s and early 1970s. It includes shared housing, eco-villages, land trusts, income-sharing communities, co-ops, spiritual communities and those organised around a specific cohort of society.

L'Arche

An example of an intentional community founded around a specific cohort is L'Arche. Founded in France in 1964, it now has 156 communities established in 38 countries around the globe.[40] These are communities of volunteers who live with people with a disability. Unlike a group home, the residential setting is based on "mutual relationships of friendship, care and compassion between people with and without an intellectual disability. These friendships are lived out through sharing daily life, with all its joys and struggles, opportunities for learning and celebration"[41] L'Arche communities are not built on the paid provision of service. L'Arche aims to promote what people with disabilities give to the general community as well as celebrate their gifts. Although L'Arche has been somewhat tarnished by the revelations of inappropriate behaviour of its founder, its work continues due to the positive change it has made in the lives of both the volunteers and the residents who have a disability.

Saint Joseph's House of Prayer

Another intentional community was Saint Joseph's House Prayer, established in a vacant orphanage/children's home owned by the Catholic Diocese in Goulburn NSW, Australia. The community cared for the buildings and surrounding land on the banks of the Wollondilly River. The community was established with the support of the Catholic Diocese. The Diocese had been inspired by one of the aims of Vatican II for lay people to take up a bigger role in the church. It was Australia's first House of Prayer. The original members were a community of lay women led by Sue Gordon.

Over time, the community included men, families and children. While this provided the church with people who would maintain the property, it also provided the community of Goulburn with a substantial resource that added to the life of the community and provided deep connection amongst the members of the St Joseph's community, local congregations and the greater community. After almost 30 years of service, the community closed in 2005.

The House of Prayer maintained regular times of prayer and devotion throughout the day according to the Catholic lexicon, but much greater than this devotion to prayer was the service it provided to the greater community of the area.

The community of St Joseph's was made up of a core group of members. They lived on the property, participated in the regular devotional activities, cared for the land the building was established on and provided pastoral care for those who passed through the House of Prayer. The members also participated in the local congregations of the Catholic Church. They lived in community with each other and reached out to the local community.

As well as conducting times of devotion they conducted various ecumenical retreats and maintained close contact with similar communities throughout Australia. For example, they maintained a close relationship with L'Arche in the early days of its work in Australia.

They also fulfilled other important functions for the community of Goulburn. Their celebrations of important religious events throughout the year became events to be attended. Easter was a lively reverent celebration of the Stations of the Cross, while Christmas was a colourful celebration of the birth of Jesus including a Passion Play where Mary and Joseph would arrive on a donkey from the farm that formed part of the land the community of St Joseph's cared for. These celebrations of high points in the Catholic religious calendar attracted both members of local Catholic congregations and other people from the local community.

The House of Prayer was where both strangers and those needing a halfway house in their healing process were welcomed with open arms. They were invited to stay as long as they needed. It became a place where they could share their healing journey as well as find the respite they needed from the outside world. People were healing from lifelong trauma, others were finding a way through psychological problems, there were people with disabilities and people with addiction problems seeking help.

It also provided a place where musicians and artists could meet and find time/space to work on their creative endeavours. There was always music.

Although the House of Prayer is no longer in existence, its impact is still felt by those who participated in its life and passed through its doors on their journey of healing.

Party in the Park

Lilly lives in a regional city in the north of Australia. Near her home is a large park. The park has historical links to the sugar industry. It also houses a botanic garden, water park, an all-abilities playground, and is used by many in the community for picnics and family gatherings.

Lilly and her husband wanted to build a closer connection with their neighbours and create a greater sense of community. She had the idea to create an event in this park and call it "Party in the Park". She approached the local council about such an event. She found that if it were a formal event, she would need insurance, to conduct risk assessments, and to lodge written applications with the council which would more than likely attract a hefty fee. But if it was an informal gathering of families, then none of those requirements would apply.

Lilly invited her neighbours to a party in the park. The idea was that everyone would come to the park and simply join together for a group picnic. Members of her church brought food to share. Lilly and her husband added to the concept by organising some activities such as face painting, games and craft activities for children and families in the park at the same time.

On the day of the event, almost all of those invited attended the party in the park. Lilly also invited anyone else in the park at the same time to join them. The event was a huge success.

Others liked what she was doing and started coming along to help Lilly and her husband. One of Lilly's friends also held her daughter's birthday party as a party in the park. While it was a private birthday celebration, others in the park were invited to share in the celebration. It had the added attraction of cupcakes and party activities.

Since then, Lilly, her husband and friends have organised more parties in the park. They have helped her neighbours to get to know each other and make deeper connections, adding to the growing social capital between Lilly and her neighbours.

Lilly showed leadership by connecting her neighbours in a simple and fun activity. These parties are informal events that use the gifts and skills of Lilly and her husband in organising a fun activity that was open to everyone. They also leverage the availability of a physical council asset via the usage of the park.

Busy and Gifted Connectors

It should come as no surprise that many who work in community engagement or community development are gifted at building networks and making connections with others in their local community.

Mission Australia is the backbone organisation for a Collective Impact project in Cairns South in Far North Queensland. Kylie worked as part of the backbone team for the project called Cairns South Together. The team fulfils a number of functions, including:

- Working with the steering committee to develop a guiding vision and strategy;
- Supporting activities that align with the vision and strategy;
- Data collection and how data is used;
- Community engagement and building networks to support the project;
- Supporting the development of policy;
- Developing resources for the future sustainability of the project.[42]

Kylie has been a long-term member of the local community and has established broad networks. This gift of connection is something she brought to her job from her outside-work life. It is part of who she is.

Kylie has lived in a number of places and wherever she has resided she has made strong connections with people and is always willing to provide information to help others in making similar connections. She is one of those people who seems to know everyone and is always willing to help people make connections with others. She is a connector. One of those people you can always rely on to know who to contact to meet any request.

She was invaluable in connecting members of Cairns South Together with the best people to assist in the development and completion of aligned activities. Without these skills, the Collective Impact project would have not progressed to where it is now. Her skills have been central to the development and progress of Cairns South Together. Although she might not be identified as a leader, she provided servant leadership to the project and those she encounters. Kylie is a local leader and a connector who understands that relationships are central to making connections and building community.

Another gifted connector in her community describes how this works for her: "I was thinking about it just recently when, in the same day, I had one friend ask me if I knew of other children who would be just right to join a community group they run because they don't really have those connections but knew that I would. The same day I had another friend ask me if I knew anyone who could help them with something totally random... and I didn't, but I knew just who to ask. Later that week, I had a day where a simple trip to the shops meant I bumped into half the people I know, or so it seemed and each of them contributed something valuable to conversations about community whether they realised it or not. It just flows. I love that about myself, I can't really remember when it started being a personality trait of mine, I wasn't always this way but I do love it and enjoy helping others."

This is what leadership looks like in a community. It rises up when it is needed and retreats once the task is complete. It is about serving others, not our own ego.

Lockdown Locals

Cara O'Dowd is an artist and professional photographer living in the western suburbs of Sydney. She is known for her work in fashion photography and portraits.

In June 2020, Sydney entered a lengthy period of lockdown as a response to the COVID-19 pandemic. It lasted for 106 days. This lockdown had a major impact on local businesses and communities.

People had to maintain "social distancing" of 1.5 metres from each other and community members were restricted to movement within a 5-kilometre radius of where they lived. This meant that Cara was no longer in a position to pursue her career.

In July, a month after lockdown restrictions came into force, Cara took matters into her own hands. Unable to work, she decided to create a temporary studio on the footpath outside her home. She set up a sheet from one of the beds in her house as a backdrop. She took portrait photographs of locals by inviting them into her "studio" as they passed by. She then also gifted each person a copy of their portrait. This was an act of kindness. Her husband and child acted as her photographic assistants.

The lockdown was an incredibly difficult time for the residents of Sydney. Businesses closed down, some never opened again, people felt isolated and some communities were separated from their families due to them living more than 5 kilometres away. Word quickly spread throughout Cara's suburb. People started using the one hour of outdoor exercise that they were authorised to have to visit Cara and have their photographs taken.

But the project didn't end there. With the permission of property owners, Cara and some supporters created a local art installation of the black and white photographs in large poster. These posters were placed on the side walls of cafes, houses and other infrastructure around the suburb. This created an art trail for locals to follow during their daily allotment of outside exercise time. This project helped to ease the stress of the lockdown, create connection between people and build a strong community.

The last step in the project was to compile the photographs into a coffee table book. This provided the community with a physical reminder of their time in lockdown and reminded them of what a valuable service Cara performed for her community.[43]

I chanced upon a copy of this book on a trip to meet a friend. I arrived early and got off the train. Near the train station was a barber shop. Not just an ordinary barber shop but a lively place to visit. Locals were sitting out the front talking to the barbers and the owner. While waiting for my turn and listening to the loud RnB music playing, I saw *Lockdown Locals* on a table and started browsing through it. The barber told me its story and shared that the owner of the business was in one of the portraits. Even after the project has finished, it is still connecting locals and welcoming strangers like me into the community, even temporarily.

Sandown Close

Communities are different from the inside than how they appear on the outside.

Sandown Close is a long, J-shaped cul-de-sac in Woree, a suburb of Cairns in Far North Queensland, Australia. It is nestled behind the Woree Tavern. At the rear of the tavern is a large block of private land that has never been developed. For all intents and purposes, it is vacant land maintained by the management of the tavern.

Sandown Close is home to a low socio-economic community and is mentioned in the media whenever there is anti-social behaviour occurring. Headlines such as "Drunken Brawl" appear in the local media. It is locally well known for the existence of a drug house and is an area where people are afraid to go to, except to purchase illicit substances.

The elected local government councillor for the area is Cathy Zeiger. Cathy is passionate about the community she serves and has for some time wanted to see something positive happen for the residents of Sandown Close.

In 2018, Cairns Regional Council dedicated some funds towards the installation of a mural on the back wall of the car park to the tavern. It was a concrete wall covered in graffiti. This added to the image of the area as being unsafe. At the same time, the community services unit at the council proposed to work with the community during the installation of the mural.

A local artist was contracted to work with local youth in creating the mural. While it was being created, the community services team began meeting with residents and discussing how they viewed where they lived and how they would like to see the area develop within the next five years.

The council staff also conducted some background research into the area. They found the street comprised a mixture of houses and apartments with apartments being predominant. There were 100 individual accommodation units in this comparatively small area. To the surprise of the staff involved in researching and interviewing community members, they found that they weren't overly concerned with the existence of the drug house but were more concerned about other issues such as the safety of their children walking and playing in the area. They were concerned about "hoons" driving cars dangerously in the area and endangering their children. Although these street hoons may have been attracted to the area to purchase drugs, the issue to the residents was not the drugs but the immediate risk their presence presented to the safety of children.

The council worked to install traffic-calming devices to deter this type of behaviour. In addition, during their consultation with residents, council staff realised there were enough residential units to justify a footpath. This had been overlooked in previous planning for the area.

The interviews conducted with residents found that they loved living in Sandown Close. It is close to the local shopping centre for groceries and other needs, and close to public transport. The local tavern provides a meeting spot where residents "bump" into each other and make connections. There was a resident who saw himself as the "Mayor of Sandown Close". Some residents shared an interest in cooking. One resident even provided some historical context to the area and shared that in the past there was a vibrant social club at the tavern and the land behind it would host a local cricket match on Saturday afternoons in the cooler months of the year.

The council also saw an opportunity to provide much-needed and requested street trees on the verge/nature strip of the vacant land. They worked with residents to find those interested in caring for the trees until they became established.

The trees were planted in time for the opening of the completion of the mural. The council staged a party both to open the mural and recognise the residents who would care for the trees. There were a number of local services and agencies represented at the party including the local school, council, police, Crime Stoppers and other service providers.

This was an incredibly successful celebration that painted the area in a different light. Instead of being perceived as a crime-riddled community, this was a vibrant, multicultural community that cared for their neighbourhood and loved where they lived. Cathy Zeiger said at one point, "I'm in Sandown Close at night and feel safe." One of the council staff members said that the Sandown Close community was a "pleasant surprise".

Rob's Gardening Tips

Rob Pyne is an elected political leader in Far North Queensland. He has served in local government for two terms and state government for one term. A "born and bred" local, he knows his community and works to make where he lives a better place.

Rob maintains a website where he has chronicled his own social and political history in the context of Far North Queensland. He has branded himself as "The Champion of the

Underdog".[44] On the site he also passionately writes about the city where he lives and gardening in the tropics.

For anyone who has relocated from cooler climates to the tropics, particularly the Wet Tropics, gardening can be a challenge. The plants you are familiar with either don't grow or only flourish in a different part of the year. For example, for those in mild climates, tomatoes grow in the summer months but they grow best in the dry season (i.e., the winter months) in the Wet Tropics. This is only the first of the surprises about gardening in the tropics.

Rob has provided a comprehensive guide to growing plants, particularly for food, in the Wet Tropics. His guide covers tropical fruit, tropical vegetables, tropical herbs, indoor plants, growing your own food, composting and seed collecting, among other topics.

He has provided this information free of any charge to his community. This is especially important in the context of climate change where many of the fruits and vegetables we buy travel great distances before they reach our table. Growing our own produce not only reduces this unnecessary cost but also reduces greenhouse emissions produced by packaging and transportation. In a high cost of living era, producing our own food also adds to our own sustainability.

Rob's simple action gives back to his community and helps to make it stronger.

Rebuilding Our Communities

These few brief stories about community members working to build and rebuild their communities show that it is often in the small actions that we show our greatest acts of leadership. Often these small, sometimes quirky actions lead to the greatest changes and the strongest communities.

For some, these actions are easy to do but for many, we have become isolated from each other. We find it hard to reach out to others, are afraid to welcome strangers in our midst and often live in fear. The good news is that much of this is a perception that can be changed. One of the problems is that we often don't know where to start. Fortunately, many local government authorities, agencies and other community members have compiled lists of tips and ideas to connect with others without feeling we are invading their privacy. Some of these tips are as simple as saying hello as you walk past people in the street. Even a quick smile is a starting point or waving at our neighbours as we drive past them on our way to work. To make this even simpler, I have included a list of simple activities anyone can do to connect and get to know their neighbours. This list can be found in the Appendix at the back of the book.

The Power of Community in Healing

Community is our place of healing. When we are surrounded by others who support us, we are in a better position to deal with the effects of our trauma and work on its healing.

The number and quality of social connections aid in our healing. The daily, ongoing interactions with others provide us with opportunities to revisit our trauma in a controlled and measured way. "Because it is through controllable, brief revisits that the sensitised system can slowly, painfully be 'reset'. Ideally, thousands of such therapeutic moments can be provided by the therapeutic web of loving, sensitive people in your life."[45]

These brief encounters we have with each other are part of the key to our healing. Without a connected, strong and loving community surrounding us, such healing is not possible. This is not to say that therapeutic interventions are not important. These provide us with a way to rewire our brains to respond to our trauma in healthier ways, but it is in community life where we do the hard work of healing. "With things that are very hard to deal with, you don't want to talk about the pain or loss or fear for forty-five minutes nonstop. You want to talk with a really good friend for maybe two or three minutes about some aspect of it. When it gets too painful, you step back, you want to be distracted. And maybe you want to talk more later on. It is the therapeutic dosing that really leads to healing. Moments. Fully present, powerful but brief."[46]

Crime Prevention

In this section, we will briefly discuss the prevention of crime, alternative approaches we could be implementing and an example of one community taking a different approach to crime.

CHAPTER 8:

Lies, Damn Lies and Statistics

No discussion of trauma, brain development and community would be complete if we didn't mention crime and anti-social behaviours. There are several social, economic and psychological factors driving crime, with trauma playing a contributing role.

I guarantee that every edition of my local newspaper will contain discussions of crime…youth crime in particular. Most of these articles are incredibly negative and only serve to raise fear and build a perception that our community is an unsafe place to be. The same phenomenon is present in other news sources such as television news broadcasts and current affairs programs. This media focus provides a feedback loop that continually reinforces the fear narrative. At the same time, the political class and their parliamentary representatives will enter a competition as to which political party will be seen as being "hardest on crime". This results in increasingly more punitive sentences, even for minor offences.

The problem is that the harder governments go on crime, the more punitive laws become, the more the problem seems to grow. This is then once again amplified by both traditional media and social media. Both will scream about the growth in crime and how unsafe our cities, suburbs and towns are. We are shown stories of community members being interviewed following their homes being broken into, photographs and videos of car crashes after cars have been stolen, and people reporting on social media about how crime-ridden their local suburb or town is. I guarantee that a brief examination of the media over the past twenty or so years would show the same situation. We would find similar stories and concerns going back over this time period. Our memories are very short. Perhaps one of the contributing factors is the prevalence of access we now have to news. A generation or so ago, a newspaper may have been read in the morning or evening, a radio news bulletin heard during the day and a television news broadcast at night. However, the advent of technological devices and social media has given us greater access to constant news and rumours. News has gone from being broadcast on an hourly basis at best to us now being in a constant 24/7 cycle of news at our fingertips.

Before we interrogate the statistics and research on crime, it is important to understand that crime statistics, like any set of statistics, can be interpreted in a number of ways. For example, an increase in the number of incidents could mean an increase in that particular criminal activity or it could mean that police are targeting that crime category more successfully and therefore making more arrests. At the same time, it could represent a change in government policy and legislation being implemented by both the police and court system. It could also mean that more people are committing those crimes or a smaller group of people are more active. The devil is in the detail and our own perspective, experiences and internalised beliefs will impact how we interpret these figures. It should also be kept at the front of our minds that crime statistics are usually retrospective. While they may indicate an issue, they are detailing the situation in previous months and years. They may be a good indicator and useful in lobbying for political intervention, but they tell us about the past and this may not necessarily reflect the current situation.

Youth Crime

In January 2023, the Australian Productivity Commission released figures detailing youth in detention for the 2021-22 period. During that time, Queensland topped all Australian states with the number of youth in detention and/or under supervision orders. There was an average of 287 young people in detention on any given night, with Indigenous young people being disproportionately represented. Approximately 10% of the Queensland population of young people identify as Indigenous, yet over two-thirds of those in detention were Indigenous.[47] Overall, this accounts for 100,425 nights spent in detention by children in Queensland with 65,298 of these being Indigenous youth in detention.

This high number of young people in detention represents a major cost to the people of Queensland, not only in lost opportunity for these young people but also in terms of the economic cost of $162 million dollars each year (or over $1,800 per child per day).

Apart from detention, 1,347 young people in Queensland were under supervision orders every day of the year. In simple terms, there are two types of supervision orders. One is made at the release of a young person from detention and is called a "Supervised Release Order". Under this type of order, the Queensland government aims for the young person to serve the last 30% of their sentence in the community under supervision. The young person must not break the law, must report regularly to a youth justice officer, must attend any programs recommended by the officer, must comply with the officer's directions, must notify any change of address and not leave Queensland without permission. If the young person breaches the supervision order, they could find themselves back before the court and back in detention.[48] Those under the age of 13 found guilty of committing an offence may find themselves under an "Intensive Supervision Order".[49] This is usually only ordered for those who have previously offended and aims to provide supports to reduce the risk of reoffending. It places similar restrictions on the child as a Supervised Release Order.

Remember, these detention figures are the figures for youth crime and not offences conducted by adults. Even more disturbing is that the figures indicate over half of those released from supervision will reoffend within the next 12 months.

Under pressure from both the media and the parliamentary opposition, the response from the Queensland government has been to create even tougher laws with higher penalties. For example, under new laws, the maximum prison sentence for car theft is 10 years. Additionally, two more youth detention centres are planned to be constructed. The Queensland Premier boasted that Queensland now has the toughest youth crime laws in Australia. With the state already having the highest number of young people in detention in Australia, it is obvious that these numbers will rise over the coming years. This situation reminds me of the old joke about the definition of insanity: "doing the same thing over and over again and expecting a different result".

For the Queensland government, this stance has represented a major turnaround in policy since 2019. The minister at the time stated that a punitive approach would only result in reoffending: "If we persist with a 'lock them up and throw away the key' approach with our young people, [reoffending] is exactly what will happen. There is an almost 100% chance that young people will reoffend."[50] At the time, the Queensland government was implementing policies informed by research, evidence and expert opinion, but it has now almost abandoned that approach to adopt a more punitive one favoured by their opponents and media commentators.

The situation is similar in many other states in Australia and I consider it to be reflected in other Western societies.

There must be a better way. Thankfully there is.

A Perception or a Reality?

While I am not a criminologist, I have worked in a number of communities on community safety issues for almost twenty years. Over this time, it became obvious that the perception of crime is not a reflection of the real situation and often may not be reflected in crime statistics. The more a situation is promoted through traditional media and social media, and pursued by the political class, the more we will consider it is a growing issue and a problem requiring immediate attention. It is not dissimilar to thinking about red cars and then noticing more red cars on the highway.

Please be reassured that I do not doubt that stories of home invasions, car theft and increased violence are frightening and I certainly empathise with victims of crime. My own home has been broken into in the past. I can understand and appreciate the feelings of vulnerability and the drive for some justice following the event. I do not want to minimise the fact that any crime is harmful, only that the situation is not as extreme as we are led to believe. I also do not deny the real fear felt by those with perceptions of high crime and the great distress generated by this perception. When this level of fear takes hold, it can result in the person becoming fearful of even venturing outside their homes at various times of the day. This reinforces the fear and results in the person feeling a greater sense of isolation and loneliness. It has the effect of shutting them off from their neighbourhood and community.

The Queensland Sentencing Advisory Council released a report in early 2023 into the sentencing of young people under the age of 13.[51] The report, covering the period 2019/20 to 2021/22, found that less than 10% of those sentenced were aged 10–13. Most of those were sentenced for property offences and the number sentenced for these offences had dropped. In fact, the number of youths under the age of 14 sentenced was lower than for any time in the past 10 years. If there was an increase in the number of offences committed, then other contributing factors were at play. One of these potential contributing factors may be that while the number of offences being committed may have increased, they could have been committed by the same group of young people. This is the cohort of repeat offenders who return to court over and over again. While this is a small number, there is a likelihood that it will increase with harder sentencing. Increasing the population in detention can only risk growing the number of repeat offenders. For example, if the cohort of repeat offenders in this age group sits at 10% of those sentenced and 300 were sentenced to detention, then 30 of these would be repeat offenders. However, if the number sentenced to detention increases to 500, then 50 would most likely be repeat offenders. The greater the number in detention, the greater the number of potential reoffenders who will continue to drive up crime statistics and add to the increased level of fear felt in the community. It's a vicious cycle.

CHAPTER 9:

A Just Way Forward

There are alternative pathways to addressing issues around crime other than an overly punitive approach. This is particularly the case when we are looking at many comparatively minor criminal acts committed out of a person's own personal trauma. It is understandable that a victim of crime would want the perpetrator of the criminal act to suffer some type of consequence, but if it is only a punishment and the person is further traumatised, then nothing is achieved except for our own personal sense of revenge and the increased likelihood that the person will reoffend. In this instance, we are not talking about violent crimes, although that offender would still benefit from some of the treatments for trauma and other just ways of addressing their acts and behaviours.

ACEs and Crime

There is a strong relationship between adverse childhood experiences and involvement in the criminal justice system. People arrested, charged and found guilty of a criminal offence have a much higher likelihood of having experienced trauma in their childhoods than others in the general population. While much of the research in this area has been conducted in the United States of America, more informal evidence from other countries validates this earlier research. For example, prison surveys conducted in the United Kingdom reveal that offenders have often experienced physical and emotional abuse as children, witnessed domestic violence, have a history of interactions with child-protection services, have a family member in prison, and a history of suspension and expulsion from school. These are all risk factors associated with future criminal behaviour.[52]

Additionally, those who experience more than one ACE have a higher chance of engaging in risk- taking behaviours with the potential for these behaviours to lead to involvement with the criminal justice system. Significantly, the Welsh ACEs Study reported that those with four or more ACEs were: 14 times more likely to be a victim of violence in the past year; 15 times more likely to be engaged in violent behaviour in the last year; and 20 times more likely to have spent time in detention and prison in their lives than a person with one ACE.[53]

At this point, it is wise to exercise some degree of caution. This is not a causal relationship (i.e., a person who has experienced a high number of ACES will not necessarily become involved in criminal behaviour). But there is a higher probability that this may occur. This risk of it happening is increased.

What Can We Do?

Youth crime is a complex issue requiring a coordinated approach to reduce it, let alone eliminate it. No one element will eliminate youth (or any other) crime from our society. It takes a comprehensive and coordinated approach to make a real difference. A policing solution alone will not provide the result we all want to see. This is a complex social issue requiring not just a criminal-justice solution but also systemic social, economic and political changes. While a period of incarceration is designed as a deterrent, it rarely operates in this way with many continuing to reoffend on release from detention or prison. We need a different approach.

To be successful, an approach to youth crime needs to include investment in programs for families, children and young people while addressing poverty, access to education, housing and homelessness. These programs need to be inclusive and culturally relevant. Early-intervention programs with a focus on the family are crucial. Building a strong and supportive family unit is one way to reduce the incidence of childhood trauma and reduce the likelihood of a young person becoming involved in criminal behaviour. Examples could be programs to develop parenting skills; home-visitation programs targeting children at greater risk of experiencing childhood trauma; early childhood education programs that are accessible and readily available; and school-based programs targeting truancy and school suspensions/expulsions while building the child's social and emotional coping mechanisms.[54]

One key component often overlooked by legislatures is leveraging the power of connected and strong communities. There are fantastic, untapped assets in communities waiting to be called upon to create a better world. If these assets were leveraged along with programs aimed at addressing issues of systemic inequality, then great change is possible. It is not a simple problem to solve but a problem we can address through working together. As the police often say in media conferences, "This is not something we can arrest our way out of." It takes a joint effort to create the change many are calling for.

Two key elements of any response must be the elimination or reduction of trauma experienced by a young person and the building of a supportive and responsive community. We have already discussed that the early childhood experiences of many young people contribute to the incidence of trauma in their lives and place them in a position where they are at increased risk of entering the criminal justice system. This is due to the impact of childhood trauma on the developing brain that often leaves the person with poor decision-making skills and an increased openness to risk-taking behaviour. Once they are caught up in the world of police, courts and detention, the risk of increased criminality becomes a reality. Certainly, holding a child on remand and then in detention only provides those already traumatised with additional trauma and adds to the potential for them to become further entrenched in the criminal justice system. Once released from a period of detention, they often come out not only more traumatized, but also angrier at the society and system that has failed them.

The sad thing is that the research and scientific evidence has been in front of us for so long. The ACEs Study was published in 1998 and numerous studies have been conducted since then into trauma, its impact and interventions that have an opportunity to make a difference in a person's life, including the reduction of criminality. In addition to the work on trauma, there is a large body of research into criminality, the criminal justice system and the high risk that detention does little to change a person's behaviour. Again, the evidence-based approach is frequently ignored by governments in developing their legislative agenda in relation to crime prevention. Youth crime elicits an emotional response from the community and is easily politicised with any alternative to punitive measures being portrayed as being "soft on crime".

If we, as a society, are going to address crime, then these populist calls for a "hard-on-crime" approach need to be refuted and ignored as a policy setting in favour of listening to the evidence.

A potentially productive place to start in aiming to reduce crime is to reduce or prevent the trauma experienced by a person. While trauma may never be totally eradicated, the incidence of it can be reduced. Some approaches have a greater chance of working to lessen the impact of trauma on a young person and helping them to turn their lives around. Often these approaches come at a much lower cost than incarcerating the child. But they don't have the same political and social media attraction.

Let's look at some of these alternative approaches that could be undertaken.

Treat the Trauma

Rarely is trauma taken into account when a young person's life intersects with the criminal justice system. If they are arrested, charged or placed on remand, there is likely to be no mental health assessment or even a brief discussion of the trauma the young person may have suffered. As Luke Twyford (Queensland Family and Child Commission) has stated "...responses must also address the circumstances that led young people to offend—including disengagement from education, poverty, childhood abuse, exposure to domestic and family violence, family financial stress, housing instability, drug and alcohol misuse, intergenerational disadvantage and systemic racism."[55] The systems and events creating trauma in a person's life need to be addressed. Even if trauma and past life experiences are mentioned, it is more likely that these will be in the context of the person's solicitor using the information to reduce the final penalty for the person and not for seeking interventions and programs to help heal the person.

Let's briefly refresh our minds as to why trauma is so important in the context of crime, particularly youth crime. When a person experiences an event resulting in trauma, such as an adverse childhood experience, stress can occur. If this stress is maintained for a lengthy period of time with no emotional buffering from a caregiver, the architecture and wiring of the brain can be impacted. Over time, this can result in the amygdala being over-stimulated and the hippocampus becoming less developed than it otherwise would be due to the prefrontal cortex of the brain being underdeveloped. The impact on the person will be impaired capacity for decision making, difficulty in regulating emotions and poor impulse control. This can lead to the person making poor decisions and engaging in high-risk behaviours, resulting in potential criminal or anti-social behaviour.[56]

Although the ACEs Study examined a range of traumas occurring to children under the age of 18, the first two years of a child's life are when the brain is developing the quickest and constantly rewiring itself. Trauma experienced during this time can have the greatest and potentially lifelong impact. This is the period of time when brain plasticity is at its peak. Following this period, brain plasticity slows down but has another period of intensity during early puberty. It is little wonder that young people who have experienced trauma early in life, come from an unsafe home and have poor decision-making skills will become caught up in criminal activity. Yet, trauma treatment is secondary to punishing the behaviour once the child interfaces with the police and court systems.

Involvement with the criminal justice system can add to the trauma experienced by the young person. It should be remembered that by the time a person is involved with the police, youth detention and court systems, many have already had poor experiences with their family, and found school a struggle and a place where they feel vulnerable. Many have experienced interventions from the child protection system and may have been removed from the care of their family and been in state care. Some would be on and off this merry-go-round.

They are already angry young people. The added experience of detention only increases this anger and adds additional trauma. Logically, this is not a formula to reduce or eliminate crime but to further entrench the young person on the pathway to a life of crime. For some, there may also be the potential for detention to be the safest place they can experience. If the home is unsafe or unstable and they don't feel safe on the street with their peers or are alienated from their peers, then this may be the case. This could mean increased offending to return to detention. People tend to act out their trauma in different ways.

There are a number of potential treatments for trauma that could be instigated once a child interfaces with the criminal justice system. These could include psychological interventions such as trauma-informed cognitive behaviour therapy and eye movement desensitization reprocessing (EMDR) therapy. EMDR is a psychotherapeutic treatment aimed at reducing the stress and distress associated with traumatic memories.[57] A range of other treatments including social treatments can also be implemented. These could include mentoring, diversionary activities and alternative educational opportunities.

There are also other trauma-informed approaches to working with youth who have committed criminal acts.[58] Upon entering detention or any type of custodial arrangement, the young person could be screened for ACEs. All staff they interact with should be educated in trauma-informed responses and approaches and be expected to respond to them from this knowledge base. Both the young person and their family should be involved in any planning around the person's time in detention, particularly in regard to any actions that aim to eventually restore the person to being a productive member of society. A change in the culture of detention facilities also needs to occur. Often these places are sterile and punitive environments. The culture needs to change from one of punishment to one of treating the young person with dignity. Detention facilities should not be standalone institutions. They need to be working in a proactive partnership with community services, child-protection agencies, psychologists and other professionals in working with the young person so that detention provides an opportunity for real reform to occur in that young person's life. A review of detention approaches could also be made to examine alternative arrangements for a person to serve their sentence.[59]

However, if governments do not have the focus on healing the trauma but a more punitive hard-on-crime position instead, such intervention is unlikely to occur as the system will not exist for these measures to be put in place. The main point is that little will change until we treat the underlying trauma and provide the appropriate environment for treatment to be performed.

Restorative Justice

If the current approach is detention and entry to the criminal justice system that has the potential to further traumatise the child, it is important we begin to look at some of the alternative approaches.

Two of these approaches are restorative justice and transformative justice. Don't let the similar titles confuse you. They are different. One is about restoring the person to society and the other is about transforming social systems that contribute to the maintenance of criminal and anti-social behaviour. In restorative justice, we are looking at how we can restore the person to society. This will often involve personal change and outline actions the person must do to restore the situation. It does not address the systemic issues contributing to the person's trauma, life situation and consequent criminal behaviour.

Transformative justice is interested in both personal transformation and the reformation of the system. The system has
often played a major role in the person both experiencing
trauma and in maintaining the situation where the individual
cannot escape from the lifestyle and influences contributing to
the criminal act.

Restorative justice is an approach that focuses on the damage
caused by crime and wrongdoing to people, relationships and
the community.[60] The aim of restorative justice is to move from
punishment and harm to the healing of individuals, relationships and communities. In practice, it brings together all parties
to discuss the criminal action, the damage the action caused and
how the situation can be repaired. These are structured interventions. There is no one way to achieve this discussion and
approaches can be quite flexible. Restorative justice is now used
in a number of different settings apart from criminal justice.
These include education, community, employment conflicts and
resolving environmental clashes.[61]

Restorative-justice approaches have much of their basis in
the worldviews of Indigenous cultures. This is best summarised
by Archbishop Desmond Tutu: "Restorative justice is characteristic of traditional African jurisprudence that is infused with 'the
spirit of ubuntu', which seeks to restore, heal or mend breaches,
imbalances and broken relationships."[62]

The approach is designed to provide reconciliation between
the offender, the victim and the community. It provides an
opportunity for the victim and the offender to come to an
agreement on what would help them both move forward. Part
of this process is for the offender to be accountable for their
actions. In restorative justice processes, the offender admits
what they have done, the victim and/or community representatives talk about the damage that has been done to them, the

offender apologises for their behaviour, publicly promises not to reoffend, and agrees to some type of restitution for their action/s and the damage done.[63]

I participated in this process when I was representing a local-government agency whose property had been vandalised by graffiti attacks. Also participating were business owners who had experienced property damage in the graffiti attack. The young person charged with vandalism sat in a circle with the victims and listened to them discuss the cost to them both personally and professionally. They spoke of how it had interrupted their business, cost them money, made them angry and feel unsafe, and what they would like to see the offender do to restore themselves to the community.

The offender then spoke about what he had done. The young person admitted his actions, apologised and discussed what would happen next. The consequence for the person was that they had to repaint the walls of the businesses they had graffitied while the business owner supervised their work. Following the meeting, a time and place was negotiated for the work to be done and the repairs were made to the satisfaction of the owner. The local government authority had already repaired the graffiti on their property as they had a policy to remove graffiti within 48 hours to reduce the incidence of further vandalism. This process made the offender accountable to the property owners, the community and themselves. It gave them an opportunity to make amends and then move on with their life without further traumatisation through the criminal justice system.

Central to this process is the willingness of the offender to participate. If the participation is based only on avoiding a court appearance or a period of detention, then it may not be a successful process. And if the person is being restored to a dysfunctional and traumatised family setting, then there is a strong likelihood that nothing will change for the person and a high chance they will once again be caught up in the cycle of offending and ongoing involvement with the criminal justice system. While restorative justice works for some, it doesn't work for all. The main problem is that many forms of restorative justice aim to rehabilitate young people back into a system that has not changed and is in essence broken. The focus is attempting to change the person to fit the system.[64]

Further along this spectrum is transformative justice. This approach has similarities to restorative justice but is interested, not only in individual changes, but also system changes. It comes from the abolitionist movement. This movement aims at questioning what safety is, how we achieve/preserve safety and what the cost is to all of us. The abolitionist perspective views prisons, police and forms of surveillance as not being able to solve our social problems. Instead, the system of social control creates harm to perpetrators of crime, victims and communities. The abolitionist approach proposes systems and cultures that promote wellbeing such as education, healthcare, housing and a connected community.[65] It has the advantage over restorative justice in removing the obstacles a person faces by changing the system that traps the young person. It breaks the vicious cycle of offending and provides positive systemic support for the person to change their lifestyle, develop necessary skills and move out of patterns that have a negative impact on them. While a transformative approach may use similar tools as restorative justice, such as conferencing, circle sentencing and the need for accountability, it has the further aim of social and systems change to create a future where crime is minimised by the positive systems in operation.

The strengths of both restorative and transformative processes are that they are inclusive and holistic, including all who are impacted by crimes. Unlike the current criminal justice system, they don't exclude victims and communities from the process of change, healing and rehabilitation. They are central to the justice process. Both restorative and transformative justice provide ways for the offender to once again become part of the community and begin the healing process.

Social Connection

It is recognised by community workers, psychologists, neurologists and a number of other professionals that community (social connection) is where we heal. We are a species driven by the need to be in groups, socialise and build relationships with each other. We need connection with each other to survive and prosper.

The power of community as a healing force is that it helps us to build resilience and gain insights into past trauma. We heal together by being connected with each other. When we are in a connected community, we are in a healthy and thriving community and find our strength from each other. As Dr Bruce Perry has said, "A healthy community is a healing community, and a healing community is full of hope because it has seen its own people weather—survive and thrive."[66] This sense of connection and belonging is a strong indicator of our mental health and wellbeing. As a place of healing, this connection can assist us in addressing past trauma and growing from the experience.

If we don't provide that connection in our homes and communities, then young people will seek it elsewhere. If they feel unsafe at home and don't have adults outside the family they can go to for support, then they may feel safer in the street with their peers. Without an adult figure they can trust and feel safe with, they may become further marginalised and disconnected from the community by seeking comfort with other young people. This will often result in risky behaviour which often ends in incidents bringing them to the attention of the police. Many have already been involved with child- protection agencies and feel alienated from their community. They are angry at the social systems that have failed them and continue to traumatise them. And it is at this point, they come in contact with the criminal justice system, often resulting in periods of detention.

However, if opportunities can be provided for young people to experience positive social connections and create caring relationships with people of all ages, they can begin the process of healing trauma. This work is often conducted through some psychological and/or medical treatment but supported through regular and informal social interactions. These ongoing social interactions provide the dose of exposure to the trauma that a person can control, reducing the distress generated by the trauma over time. And if safe places for a young person can be created where they can interact with others in an inclusive and non-judgemental environment, then we already have the social elements in place that are effective at reducing the risk of crime.

Building the Village

One of the often-used sayings in relation to early childhood development is "it takes a village to raise a child". There is great truth in these few words but one of the issues we face and the question we need to answer in relation to it is this: do we have the village to raise the child?

Over the course of the last two or three generations, our society has changed greatly. We travel further to work each day and no longer work in the same suburb or even town where we live. When we return home, we often only make contact with our immediate family or the people we share accommodation with, and we rarely venture into the streets outside our homes.

In 1984, the average Australian had nine friends they could trust and rely on. Now, this is down to five. We don't meet with our friends as frequently as we once did. Twenty years ago, we had regular weekly get-togethers with our friends. This has now dropped to fortnightly, at best. At the same time, fewer are volunteering, union members, playing organised sport or attending organised religious observances.[67]

The local places where we once connected with other people and met our neighbours are no more. The local corner stores where we could buy immediate supplies and often spend time in discussions with others are disappearing. It is rare to find one still operating. If one does still operate, we are more likely to drive to it rather than walk, forgoing the opportunity to bump into our neighbours along the way. We rarely even know our neighbours' names, children no longer play in the streets and we don't use our front yards. It is getting hard to find that village.

One of the results of this is an increased sense of isolation. Loneliness and isolation are some of the major contemporary issues facing us as a society. In 2018, the English Prime Minister appointed a Minister for Loneliness. The aim of this position was to address both social and mental health issues associated with loneliness. Out of a population of 66 million people in the United Kingdom, 9 million reported being lonely either often or all the time. Additionally, other research has shown over 200,000 older people in the UK had not had a conversation with a friend or relative for over a month.[68] Loneliness, to this extent, represents more than a mental health issue. It also impacts physical health. It can lead to conditions such as high blood pressure, heart disease, chronic inflammation and dementia. The impact of loneliness has been stated as being worse for health than smoking 15 cigarettes a day.[69]

Loneliness and isolation add to people's feelings of fear and the perception that their street is an unsafe place to be. They become fearful of even walking in their own streets. We no longer welcome the stranger into our lives, viewing those we don't know with suspicion. Social-media pages are full of posts of people reporting strangers in their street as potential criminals and being advised to report them to the police.

In healing our traumas, the sense of being part of a village (a community) is essential. When we live in a safe place, connection with others allows us to revisit our trauma in small doses that we can control and handle. Over time, revisiting trauma in this type of environment helps us to develop a more regulated stress reaction and eventually create resilience. This is all part of the healing power of the community.[70]

We need to rebuild our village. But how do we do this?

In essence, this is quite simple, but in practice it can be much more difficult as we need to counter the fear and reluctance that has developed through our neighbourhoods being socially disconnected. The rebuilding can start with saying a simple hello to people we pass in the street. But to do this we need to get out of our houses and back into our streets. Go for a walk. Greet the people you pass on your walk. If you walk at the same time each day, you will often greet the same people each day.

This is a simple way to start. There are many other actions that can be taken to help build friendships and relationships. Small interactions, such as stopping for a chat, offering to put the neighbours' bins away if they can't, and keeping an eye on their property when they are away. This is where we start to rebuild the village. It may not be easy for some of us, but these small, non-invasive actions make us vulnerable and open to others and can form the basis of friendships that can form our village.

Going further, you could invite your neighbours to a group picnic in the local park, join a local community group, volunteer for local environmental groups, join a church or find a local coffee shop and become a regular. These are all simple actions but can start the process of rebuilding our villages.

When we connect with our neighbours, we begin to develop trust between ourselves and others. These interactions are often referred to as social capital—the social connection between us, the networks we establish, our reciprocal actions towards each other and the growth of trust we experience.[71] When social capital develops, people start to care for each other and start to act out of a sense of altruism to keep their neighbourhood safe. When enough neighbours are connected, this creates a "collected efficacy" and a certain level of behaviour is expected in the street. The concept is very simple. When enough people form a connection, they start to develop informal and formal norms of behaviour. There are clear expectations of what is acceptable in that place and what is not. Neighbours will intervene when these norms are breached.

The clear result is a reduction in unacceptable behaviour. People are less likely to experience violence and crime in the street.[72]

There are numerous lists available of actions people can undertake to connect with their neighbours. A simple Google search will reveal a number of these. One such list is found in the Appendix at the back of the book.

The Assets of Youth

Often young people are viewed as a problem in our society. There are daily news articles about youth crime, youth gangs and vandalism caused by juveniles. They are viewed through a lens of suspicion in shopping centres. They are noisy when they get together and this often leads to people steering clear of them as they find their noise intimidating. They often take unnecessary risks which may lead them along the path of confrontation with authorities. They can often exhibit rebellious behaviour, "thumbing their nose" at authority.

Consequently, our society has placed legislative barriers on how they can use public space. We have highly regulated public spaces to the degree that it is difficult for them to find somewhere to be "kids" and let off some steam without confronting some form of authority. Skateboards and bicycles are prohibited from certain locations, there are noise limitations in other places, and young people often find themselves moved on from shopping centres by security staff for one reason or another. In other words, young people are often viewed as trouble.

How easy it is to view them in a negative light. If only they could be "seen and not heard".

When we read our local newspapers, watch our local news and read social media comments, we don't see their strengths. We only see that they cause trouble, commit crimes and are responsible for vandalism and graffiti. While it might be comforting to think that this view is a rather recent one developed through youth rebelling in the 1950s and the counter-culture of the 1960s, it has been a long-standing stance from an older generation to a younger generation. We don't have to look far to see this attitude. Two of the Western world's greatest philosophers must surely take the trophy for succinctly displaying this attitude:

Around 500 BC, Socrates said: "Our youth today now love luxury; they have bad manners, contempt for authority, disrespect for older people. Children nowadays are tyrants, they no longer rise when elders enter the room, they contradict their parents, they chatter before company, gobble their food and tyrannise their teachers. They have terrible manners, flout authority, have no respect for their elders. What kind of awful creatures will they be when they grow up."

And 200 years later, Aristotle is quoted as saying: "When I look at the younger generation, I despair for the future of civilisation."[73]

These are our future business operators, entrepreneurs, writers, musicians, artists, teachers and leaders that we are labelling in this way.

It sounds so familiar, doesn't it? But it needn't be so negative.

Instead of pushing our youth away, we need to welcome them into our communities. The more we push them away, the more they are marginalised and disenfranchised, and the more their trauma goes unhealed. The village is not a village if young people are not an active part of it. We need to welcome them back with open arms. After all, the community is our healing place. If we don't do this, we continue to push them away and we create more young people at risk of confronting the criminal justice system through taking unnecessary risks. But if we view the other side of the coin, we can see that young people are one of our greatest assets. They represent the potential so many of us have lost. Young people often have a view of the world that is untainted by life's twists and turns.

They lack the scepticism that comes with age. Youth can offer us a positive vision of the future. One where anything is possible. They often see themselves as "10 ft tall and bulletproof". Indestructible. Youth offer us a creative lens to view the world through. They are unafraid to create, write, paint and bear their souls through art. With all these gifts and potential, you would think that our society would be harnessing their promise to create a better world. Unfortunately, they are often our most overlooked assets.

To truly rebuild the village, we need to include the gifts and passions offered by youth. Simply inviting them to participate in the actions of the community is a good place to start. When we overlook what they are so readily offering, we fail to build our village. Without young people, there is no village.

One of the problems we have with our contemporary communities is that we have lost the gift of hospitality and welcoming the stranger. More often than not, if we see a stranger in our street, we write about it on social media, warn people to lock up, and call the police. We don't even talk to the stranger. In essence, we need to turn this around. It is something we can easily do, or else we will continue to miss the gifts of young people. As Cormac Russell has said, "There is space and hospitality within every community for the gifts of all young people (regardless of their history or reputation) if we intentionally invite it in and make the connections. These spaces will not be found unless we actively seek them out."[74]

CHAPTER 10:

Case Study—Sanctuary Point Community Pride

This case study is an example of what can be achieved by a community when they focus on connection and celebrating the gifts and strengths they already have at their disposal. The study relates to actions to create a safe community in Sanctuary Point, NSW. When working with members of the Sanctuary Point community, the local council took a strengths-based approach influenced heavily by asset-based community development (ABCD).

Community Pride Background

Shoalhaven City Council is a local government area on the South Coast of NSW, Australia. It comprises a number of towns and villages stretching up and down the coast. The area is a popular tourist destination two hours' drive south of Sydney.

The council developed an approach to community safety through community development called Community Pride. The aim was to change the perception from one of a community operating in deficit with problems requiring external intervention to a community rich in assets and resources where community members could shape their own future.

Initially, Community Pride was used as a strategic response to reports of anti-social behaviour in one suburb. The residents of that community were feeling disconnected and felt the location needed to improve its image. Council's community development team met with interested community members to discuss their issues.

The council advocated for the community to try an asset-based community development (ABCD) approach to their concerns. With this approach, there is a focus on what the community already has: the physical assets; the gifts, talents and abilities of its residents; the stories and culture of the area; the local community groups; the government agencies already present in the area and the connections between people. The aim is to connect and mobilise these assets to create change. It is a process driven by the community.

Interested residents met with council staff and created an asset map of the area. This initially contained details of physical assets and infrastructure. Meetings continued with residents taking ownership quickly and choosing the Community Pride name.

Success on this first Community Pride project led the council to establish it as a way to work with local communities. A policy was developed and the approach was used in a number of other local communities. One of these was Sanctuary Point.

Sanctuary Point

Sanctuary Point is a small community on the shores of St George's Basin (in close proximity to Jervis Bay). It is about 25 km from Nowra, NSW.

At the 2021 Census, it had a population of 7,874. Although this is a small population figure, Sanctuary Point is one of a number of interconnected suburbs in the area and for a visitor, it is sometimes difficult to tell where one suburb ends and another starts.

Housing development in Sanctuary Point dates back to the 1960s. There was rapid growth in the 1990s and steady growth since then.

Demographically, it has a large population of seniors and a low proportion have tertiary qualifications. High school completion rates are also low. In addition, Sanctuary Point has an unemployment rate that is often higher than the national unemployment rate. It can be easy to label the area as disadvantaged, but like anywhere, it has significant assets and resources.

Sanctuary Point Community Pride Background

In July 2009, a safety audit was conducted on Francis Ryan Reserve. This is a sporting ground situated behind the Sanctuary Point shopping strip. A service road runs between the sporting ground and the back of the shops. This road provides entry to a car park and is used for deliveries to the shops. The report was conducted by NSW Police but was not actioned.

In 2010, there was mounting community interest and political pressure for the council to action the audit. The council responded by assigning their youth development officer to action it. This report contained a number of actions related to crime prevention through environmental design. This is a crime-prevention approach based on making changes to the design, environment and physical infrastructure of an area to lessen the likelihood of a criminal action occurring.

In January 2011, a local resident began producing a newsletter. Initially, this newsletter focused on maintenance and safety issues with an emphasis on viewing Sanctuary Point as a forgotten village by the local council. No distinction was made in the newsletter between public and private land with the inference that it was all the council's responsibility. The newsletter was published on a monthly basis. Although critical of the council, the writer of the newsletter and other residents showed an interest in partnering with them to make some changes to the amenity of the area by removing graffiti and conducting maintenance.

Community Meeting

Community members had been raising concerns about crime to the council, police and other authorities for a few months. With a sense that the community was becoming frustrated with the responses they were receiving, the council decided to coordinate a public meeting to try and address the concerns. This meeting was held in a local community centre in June 2011.

The purpose of the meeting was to discuss what positive outcomes could be achieved by the community working together to build a safer community. The meeting was addressed by the police, council and community members.

The council discussed the work they were doing in the area to maintain council infrastructure and to reassure those present that Sanctuary Point was not a forgotten village. The police then outlined crime statistics, perceptions of crime and the need to report crime. The meeting then broke into small groups to discuss the following:

- Strengths/assets of the area, including individual strengths;
- Policing/crime issues;
- Youth issues;
- Ideas.

People rotated through these groups so that they had the opportunity to contribute to the discussion for each group. This assisted in reducing the opportunity for one person to dominate the discussion and derail the process.

Following the small group discussions, the meeting regrouped and, after some further discussion, decided to set up a committee to oversee the development of the ideas produced.

Beginning

This was the second community where the council utilised the Community-Pride approach. It was still a fresh concept and council officers were convinced that if the community could identify, mobilise and connect its assets, then the focus on crime would diminish with a stronger community developing and a new narrative replacing that of crime.

A Council community development officer was allocated to convene/facilitate the meeting until the community group felt they were ready to take ownership. This officer was supported by other officers from other sections of the council to assist in addressing issues outside the knowledge of the community development unit. The period of council providing this level of support to the committee was much longer than first anticipated. Council provided ongoing support to the committee for almost two years. It was fortunate the officer allocated to facilitate the task had the gift of patience and displayed significant skills in building relationships within the committee.

Meetings were held with the committee on a monthly basis. For a lengthy period of time, the group struggled to find its focus. A number of issues were discussed. At first, the meetings became sidetracked by insurance and appropriate email correspondence discussions. These difficulties were increased by members of the group not having experience in meeting procedures. This storming phase of group development proved to be problematic and extended for many months. For those involved, it felt like the project would fail with the coordinator of the community development unit at the council considering abandoning the project. This would have occurred if the officer meeting with the committee had not advocated strongly for the work to continue.

Some Success

Although the committee was struggling to find its purpose, its action on graffiti provided some success. The council supplied materials for volunteers to remove graffiti from council assets. The writer of the newsletter gathered other residents together to work on graffiti removal. This resulted in a large reduction in the incidence of graffiti tags around the local area.

The council maintained its commitment to the project throughout these early, difficult months. The regular attendance of staff at meetings created contact and liaison between council staff and community members. This assisted in building relationships and helped in informing the community of the work the council was completing in their area. This information flow also assisted in countering the perception that Sanctuary Point was the "poor cousin" of other villages in the area. One of the early actions of the committee was the production of a community survey. Council assisted the committee in formulating the survey and had resources available to collate the results. By the end of the first 6 months, the group survey was ready to distribute to the community.

The Survey

The survey covered the following matters: shopping precinct use; likes/dislikes of the area; suggested improvements; concerns/issues; additional facilities; priorities for improvements to the shopping precinct; the location of planned skate park; CCTV installation and any requests from residents to join the committee.

175 responses were received with 90 being from people over 60 years of age. While this proportion may have skewed the results, it provided some important information for both the committee and the council as to potential future actions.

Survey Results

The survey provided the following information:

Likes:

- Country lifestyle;
- Easy access;
- Less traffic;
- Affordable housing;
- Geographical location;
- Village setting;
- Convenience of facilities;
- Friendly community;
- Access to water.

Those responding had recognised some of the assets of the area that added to the amenity and liveability of Sanctuary Point.

Dislikes:

- Crime/drug use/graffiti;
- Not feeling safe;
- No police;
- Unruly young people;
- Unsightly shops;
- Potholes in the car park;
- Rubbish/unmaintained areas;
- Tainted image;
- Excessive speed/noise;

- Anti-social behaviour;
- Lack of kerbs and gutters;
- Pedestrian conflict with bikes/skateboards near shops;
- Lack of cheap, accessible public transport.

This represented a range of issues for community members. There was some consideration by council staff that some of these dislikes related more to rumours of anti-social events rather than reflecting the facts of the situation.

Priority Issues:

- Police-response time;
- Feeling unsafe;
- Lack of opportunities for young people;
- Attractiveness of public areas;
- Village pride;
- Lack of walkways;
- Drainage/road maintenance;
- State of shops/car park;
- Anti-social behaviour;
- Appearance of private dwellings;
- Road safety;
- Medical services.

Suggested Improvements:

- Clean up overgrown nature strips/road verges/behind shops and improve drainage;
- Provide social/recreational options, e.g., a men's shed, activity/recreation for young people;
- Improve/more public toilets;
- Improve entrance into Sanctuary Point;
- Provide more bins/hard-rubbish collection;

- More public transport;
- Improve skate park;
- More walkways;
- A bigger library;
- Clean up vacant and overgrown properties;
- Kerbs and guttering;
- More bench seating.

Concerns and Suggestions Regarding Incivility:

- Security patrols;
- Clean up litter/graffiti;
- More speed-control devices;
- Provide land for a police station;
- Stop motorbikes using council reserves;
- More ranger patrols;
- More alcohol-free areas;
- Educate young people on community values;
- Behaviour;
- Noise;
- Litter;
- Graffiti.

Crime Suggestions:

- Police station. There was a preference for one operating on a 24-hour-per-day, seven-days- per-week basis, rather than being staffed only during business hours.
- Increased police patrols;
- 83% of those completing the survey were in favour of CCTV being installed at the shopping precinct.

However, crime statistics over a 2-year period (2012/13) for the shopping strip did not reflect the issues stated in the survey.

The statistics showed only 50 reports of malicious damage (decreasing rapidly during 2013). There were 10 assaults and 9 reports of break and enter. These statistics were quite low.

The main problem was assessed as a perception of crime and the presence of incivility rather than crime.

Sanctuary Point Place-Making Action Plan

Shoalhaven City Council developed a place-making action plan in partnership with the committee and other members of the community. One of the council officers attending the group on a regular basis was from the strategic planning section of the council and had recent training in place-making planning. As well as the Sanctuary Point Community Pride committee, a large number of other local organisations and agencies were consulted, and a cross-section of additional council staff were involved in formulating the plan.

Council viewed the plan as being a necessary response to community concerns and perceptions about the liveability of the area. They also wanted to counter the view of council inaction in terms of prioritising asset construction and maintenance in Sanctuary Point.

The plan was comprehensive and comprised short-term, medium-term and long-term priorities. It included priorities for the whole community, not just the shopping precinct.

Prior to and during the development of the plan, council had already been working on a number of local projects including:

- A community safety audit;
- Security-camera investigations;
- Graffiti removal/deterring investigations;
- Higher levels of public-reserve maintenance;
- Paradise Beach Road private car parking improvements

for Sanctuary Point Village Centre. This is a car park at the front of the shopping precinct. There are numerous owners of the various shops in the shopping precinct. They all have responsibility for the maintenance of the car park. Repairs to the car park require negotiations with all these owners. The high number of shop owners and the difficulty in negotiating a solution to the car-park issues with them was the main reason the car park had fallen into disrepair over a number of years.

- Bay and Basin Skate Park investigations;
- Sanctuary Point Community Pride resourcing;
- Paradise Beach Road school crossing upgrade investigations;
- Police-station investigations;
- Sanctuary Point Men's Shed investigations;
- Temporary fencing of Francis Ryan Reserve.

The Sanctuary Point place-making plan was formally adopted by Shoalhaven City Council in October 2013.

Group Cohesion

Working on the survey helped the group to start finding a focus. This cohesion was strengthened by the contribution the committee made to the place-making plan.

The survey and the place-making plan provided the committee with enough confidence to embark on their first public event. With this new confidence, they began planning and facilitating the "Spring into Sanctuary Point" community event. Its aim was to promote the positives of the area. "Spring into Sanctuary Point" gave the committee an identity. The event was planned to be an expo of all that was good about living in Sanctuary Point. Stalls were to come from organisations throughout the community, with the event including food and entertainment. This first event was held in September 2012. The first Spring into Sanctuary Point was an incredibly successful event and it has been held in subsequent years with the only disruptions being during the COVID-19 pandemic.

In October 2012, Sanctuary Point Community Pride became an incorporated association and received funding from the Bendigo Community Bank to conduct community-building activities. Subsequently, a bank account was opened in October 2012 and a letterhead was designed.

Growth and Independence

The organising of the expo event helped the group become more independent. This growth towards independence was reflected in a petition (organised by a group member) against a proposed 8% council rate rise. This petition showed the committee had become truly independent of the council and had the confidence to advocate on their own behalf.

There was a noticeable increase in maintenance and safety-issue requests made to the council. A representative of the Sanctuary Community Pride commenced attending the safer community action team (SCAT) meetings. These were community safety/crime prevention meetings sponsored by the council.

Sanctuary Point Community Pride commenced applying for funding for events and facilities, including applying to the Port Kembla Port Fund to provide funds for a police station.

The group also partnered with the Bendigo Bank, council and the Department of Sport and Recreation to install a fitness station at Paradise Beach Reserve.

In addition, they now operate a community garden, have worked to establish a "Learn to Ride" facility for children to safely learn to ride bicycles and have established the Sanctuary Point Men's Shed.

The group has moved from a reliance on others to make a better community to working with others and valuing/connecting the assets of the area. They have maintained this as part of their positive core focus. From their website: "Sanctuary Point Community Pride Inc. works to build on the assets of an area, to point to the good things and work to build pride. We look at ways to improve the quality of life for all residents, young and old alike, supporting neighbourhood self-reliance through community-based problem-solving, neighbourhood-oriented services and public and private cooperation."[75]

This has been a successful ABCD project with the aim of the council supporting and then stepping back once the community was ready to take ownership of the committee and associated projects.

The Village in Action

In this section, we move on to look at what our community (our village) looks like in action and what this means for those healing from trauma.

CHAPTER 11:

It Takes a Village…Have We Got the Concept of Family Right?

It is guaranteed that politicians will at some time refer to "family values" or even "traditional-family values". In 2021, Dominic Perrottet became the Premier of New South Wales in Australia. In his maiden speech as Premier, he said: "But I'll also be a family Premier, focusing on how we can make life better for working families. Living the liberal values of opportunity, aspiration and hard work."[76] Similarly, British Prime Minister David Cameron said in 2014: "It's family that brings up children, teaches values, passes on knowledge, instils in us all the responsibility to be good citizens and to live in harmony with others."[77]

Both quotes mention "family" and what the term stands for, but both have subtle differences. The problem is that a family can mean different things to different people based on their cultural understandings and experiences. For many, family might mean the "typical" nuclear family (i.e., a small family comprising parents and children). However, this can tend to leave out those who are not heterosexual or even those who are divorced and separated. Family can mean many things and the values that come with the concept of family can also mean many things to different people.

The Australian Bureau of Statistics has defined a family as: " two or more persons, one of whom is at least 15 years of age, who are related by blood, marriage (registered or de facto), adoption, step or fostering, and who are usually resident in the same household. Each separately identified couple relationship, lone parent-child relationship or other blood relationship forms the basis of a family. Some households contain more than one family. Non-related persons living in the same household are not counted as family members (unless under 15 years of age)."[78]

While this definition is much broader than those hinted at by the quoted politicians, it could still lock out those with a different cultural understanding of what a family means. This would include many from Indigenous backgrounds.

Before we examine the differing nature of the concept of family between the contemporary dominant culture in most of the Western world and that of Indigenous communities, it is important to examine how we arrived at where we are now. In discussing family, we are moving into the territory of cultural values and inevitably this will lead to a clash of values. Please note that this will be a brief discussion and cannot possibly hope to cover the whole calamity of colonisation on the Indigenous peoples of Australia or any other colonised country. It can only paint a picture for us to base further discussions on.

The Clash of Cultures

In any clash of cultures, there often can only be one winner. One culture will generally triumph over the other and become the dominant culture. This has sadly been the case in much of the Western world. Many nations such as Canada, Australia, New Zealand and the United States were settled by colonists from England or Europe. These colonists brought their "old world" values and concepts with them. They came with a worldview in which the "enlightened" European or English colonist settlers were seen as being civilised and those Indigenous people encountered as uncivilised. The roots of racism and cultural superiority were sewn at the start of settlement.

In 1770, Captain James Cook claimed the east coast of Australia for Great Britain. Prior to Cook setting sail, he was provided with advice from the Earl of Morton, President of the Royal Society, that in encountering the Indigenous people of a place, "They are the natural, and in the strictest sense of the word, the legal possessors of the several Regions they inhabit."[79] He also had instructions from the Admiralty: "You are also with the Consent of the Natives to take Possession of Convenient Situations in the Country in the Name of the King of Great Britain: Or: if you find the Country uninhabited take Possession for his Majesty by setting up Proper Marks and Inscriptions, as first discoverers and possessors."[80]

On disembarking at Botany Bay, Cook and his party encountered the Gweagal people as the local inhabitants of the area. Cook kept journals of his voyage and we know there was some contact between the local Indigenous community and Cook's party. Overall, the Gweagal maintained their distance but sometime during the eight days Cook was at Botany Bay, shots were fired by his crew at the local inhabitants, with an elder wounded.[81] Violence was part of Australian colonial history from the very beginning.

Although it was clear the land was already inhabited by local Indigenous people and without a treaty or other agreement made between those inhabitants and the British government, Cook claimed the land for Great Britain.

When the First Fleet arrived in 1788 with their cargo of convicts, Governor Arthur Phillip was given the following instruction from the King: "endeavour by every possible means to open an intercourse with the natives, and to conciliate their affections…and if any of our subjects shall wantonly destroy them, or give them unnecessary interruption…it is our will and pleasure that you do cause such offenders to be brought into punishment according to the degree of the offence."[82] While initial interactions were reasonably cordial, this is not how relations between the new settlers and the Indigenous tribes and peoples continued. There were clashes between settlers and Indigenous groups, with the outcome being the Indigenous population being subdued, often violently, by the colonial settlers.

At the time the territory was claimed for Great Britain and when Arthur Phillip arrived with the First Fleet, there were only three legal ways that sovereignty could be claimed:

1. By conquest;
2. By treaty;
3. By occupation: acquiring the land due to there being no government or sovereign power in place (i.e., "terra nullius").[83]

Terra nullius was the approach adopted by the settling colonists. This was ratified and formally adopted by Governor Richard Burke in 1835 as the justification for settlement.

Their justification for claiming the land as terra nullius was believing that the Indigenous population did not have permanent dwellings, did not utilise agricultural practices to show they had mastery of the land and did not exhibit sovereignty over the territory. The colonial authorities judged sovereignty by comparing the Indigenous population with English society and culture. Their experience of life in England and Europe set the benchmark by which they judged other societies and cultures.

When they viewed Indigenous communities through this lens, they erroneously viewed that the Indigenous cultures did not possess the land in the same way they did. The continent was assessed as belonging to no one: terra nullius. This enabled the colonial settlers to dispossess the First Nations people and to treat them how they saw fit.

Dispossession

With the arrival of British settlers came British law and the rule of law. Under this concept, everyone was under the law, no one was above it, and all were treated equally under the law. For the Indigenous population of the land, this meant that laws were established that had little relevance to their culture and to the traditional laws and customs that governed their way of life.

With the introduction of British law, and operating through the erroneous interpretation of terra nullius, colonial governments established settlements where they decided to with little reference to the traditional inhabitants of the land and their land usage. Land grants were issued to whoever the colonial government wished to grant title and ownership to. With this distribution of land came property rights and trespass laws. In practice, this meant that the Indigenous inhabitants of a place were often locked out of their traditional lands and punished for "trespassing" and entering them. Coupled with this was the establishment of police forces who were responsible for dispersing Indigenous people and relocating them elsewhere.[84]

This dispossession was not only made possible by the concept of terra nullius and the rule of law, but also due to the English settlers having advanced technology in the form of firearms, as well as the use of horses and camels to make them mobile. This gave them an advantage over the Indigenous population they were supplanting. As more land was taken up by farmer settlers, Indigenous people were often forced to move from the country they were familiar with and had cultural links to. They were displaced and moved to live with other displaced Indigenous groups in unfamiliar geographic locations. This meant Indigenous people lost their cultural connection to the land, their kinship ties were broken and they often shared a new living environment with other Indigenous people suffering the same fate. This was state-sanctioned, forceful and often resulted in violence both from authorities and within communities.

Massacres

The colonial period in Australia was a particularly violent time. This is evidenced by the number of massacres conducted by both the colonial authorities and individual settlers. The massacre of Indigenous people in Australia follows the massacre typology developed by French sociologist Jacques Semelin.[85] The massacres were not spontaneous. They were planned events, often carried out in secret with the justification that they were a consequence of the killing of an important person or theft of property. The secret nature of these massacres has meant that they have often been overlooked in the official telling of the history of the country, but they have lived on in the retelling of events by survivors and others.

Fortunately, these massacre stories are now being collected, recorded, and sites digitally mapped in a project, *Colonial Massacres in Australia: 1788-1930*, led by Professor Lyndall Ryan AM, FAHA.[86] The exercise includes details of the site of the massacre; circumstances leading up to the massacre; the number killed in the massacre; names of both those carrying out the massacre and those killed in it and, importantly, the means of transportation for those carrying out the massacre (i.e., on foot, horseback or by camel).

For this mapping project, a massacre was defined as "the indiscriminate killing of six or more undefended people in one operation."[87] As at March 2023, over 400 massacre sites have been mapped with over 10,000 estimated deaths. Often these sites have already been identified by the names the colonial settlers had given the location: Skeleton Creek, Murdering Point, Slaughterhouse Creek, Skull Pocket and Murder Creek.

Massacres were not the only tool used in colonial Australia to control the Indigenous population.

Removal of Children

Apart from massacres, there were ongoing clashes between settlers and Indigenous people. These were often over rights to land, property, food and water. Often, this period is referred to as the "frontier wars". Dispossession and ongoing clashes resulted in social conditions in Indigenous communities being in disarray. This gave colonial authorities the opportunity to justify the removal of children from their families and other kin. The motive for this action was the enculturation of children with European values and to provide services for settlers.[88] Families were torn apart, with children raised in state-government homes or living as domestic servants. This was often done under the premise of protecting the child but also under the belief that Indigenous people needed to be blended with colonial society and assimilated into the dominant culture.

These policies of forced removal were still in existence into the 1970s and have had a severe impact on social and cultural connections. Children in these settings were dislocated from their families and this situation did not allow them to observe positive role models and parenting styles from their own culture. They often lost their language, had no connection with their heritage and lost the connection to family. This has resulted in intergenerational trauma and a level of family and community violence.[89]

The colonial period was an extremely damaging time for Indigenous people in Australia. Displacement, disconnection with the land, family and culture, and violence suffered at the hands of the settlers and government authorities meant that Indigenous communities were torn apart.

With the removal of children and displacement of Indigenous people occurring since the early years of colonisation, there are generations of families that have suffered trauma at the hands of authorities. This is a cycle of oppression that has led to trauma transmitted from generation to generation and is a contributing factor in ongoing violence in Indigenous communities.

This was a particularly violent and damaging clash of cultures between settlers and Indigenous people, with the dominant-settler culture being the victor. The concept of terra nullius was overturned by the Mabo decision of the High Court in 1992. But the damage had already been done.

Differing Concept of Family

One concept that colonial settlers brought with them from Great Britain and Europe as they spread their reach into the "new world" was that of family. Often, the colonist families were small units comprising parents, children and limited extended family. The clash of cultures between Indigenous and colonial-settler cultures has seen the colonial-family concept become the dominant model in many Western societies. The colonial impact underlies much of how our systems and authorities still operate in regard to families and child protection. In the contemporary context, this is the nuclear family of parents and immediate children only. It does not include members of the extended family, such as uncles and aunts who have a role in child-rearing practices. In Australia, for example, this cultural mode of family has informed legislation, policy and operation of approaches towards families, child rearing and child protection.

Indigenous and First Nations families functioned in a much different manner to colonial families. In many Indigenous cultures, the extended family is the norm, with the whole community having responsibility for the safety and parenting of children. This extended family could include not only immediate family but also clans, kinship connections, elders and other community leaders.[90] Indigenous concepts of family and kinship are based on a complex system that defines how and where a person fits into the community. It provides structure for ongoing relationships, the obligations people have to each other, and acceptable behaviours within the community. A child in a community such as this will know who they are related to, who they are able to marry and who they are not permitted to marry. These are communities strongly based on family, relationship to the land and to culture. While a child will know who their birth parents are, they will often refer to aunts and uncles as mother or father, and to cousins as brothers and sisters.[91] In short, this is the village to raise the child in practice.

This concept of family was unfamiliar to the colonising authorities, and Indigenous families and communities have often been viewed as being deficient in child-rearing practices. This would account for some of the historical motivation to remove children from their communities and to "assimilate" them into colonial society. Legislation, policy and procedures have been informed by the nuclear- family model. In practice, the focus on the nuclear family accounts partly for the high number of Indigenous children still removed from their families under child-protection practices.

Additionally, the impact of trauma through colonial practices is often passed from one generation to the next. This historical trauma has impacted all colonised people. It can be witnessed in high rates of unemployment, poverty, substance abuse and domestic violence. There is an over-representation of First Nations people in the criminal justice system, and higher levels of mental health conditions are present in many Indigenous communities. Much of this is due to the intentional colonial practice of separating families, disrupting communities and the destruction of culture. The only possible result is trauma.[92] The dislocation from culture and loss of connection to family through forced removal has ongoing consequences for families.

The impact of colonisation continues. We cannot separate colonialism from racism and attempts at genocide. Although countries such as Australia, New Zealand, Canada and the USA have moved on from their colonial past, its scar is still with us. One legacy of the colonial period is racism. The insidious concept that one culture or skin colour is superior to another and that the other must be repressed is destructive and creeps into daily life on a frequent basis. It's observed in young people of Indigenous heritage being watched more closely than their white counterparts when they enter a retail outlet, the racial profiling of a person by authorities due to the colour of their skin, Indigenous children still being removed from their families sometimes for things that would not draw attention if they were from the dominant white culture. It is ongoing and systematic. Until we as a society address the ongoing racism, we cannot adequately address the transgenerational trauma driving so many inequalities.

The Myth of Parenting

There are many myths about parenting. One of the biggest myths is that we are all natural parents. In reality, none of us are born with parenting skills. We largely parent the way we were parented, both the good and the bad, unless we make a determined effort to modify these practices. Addressing the impact of intergenerational trauma based on the colonisation and destruction of culture would go some way towards healing the impact of the trauma still felt by many members of Indigenous communities and improve the situation of children. But there is still the issue that successful parenting requires the support of others. The support of the village. Indigenous cultures and communities have provided us with a model for this where members of the extended family and community are all responsible for the care and development of children. However, the disruption of culture, disconnection from the land and dislocation of families makes it difficult for this model to work. This will often mean that the support and assistance of outside agencies is required for it to function. This is particularly the case if our village requires rebuilding.

In Australia, child-protection agencies are recognising the difference between the parenting model of the extended family of an Indigenous child and the nuclear family of others in the community. One practice to support traditional Indigenous-parenting approaches is that of kinship carers. These are carers who are related to the child or, due to cultural connections, are considered to be family or close to the family. They could include uncles, aunts, other relatives, close friends or someone who is a member of the child's community. Kinship carers can be appointed if the child is deemed to require the protection of the state and be removed from their family home. Child protection officers are empowered to place the child or young person in the care of a kinship carer to maintain the child's cultural identity and ensure that the child is not dislocated from family and community. This is a recognition of the cultural differences in family structure.[93]

While this is a start in the recognition of the importance of the Indigenous model of family, more can be done to examine the strengths and benefits of such an extended family in the wellbeing of the child. Some of these principles could be adopted by the wider community to enhance the wellbeing and relational opportunities for all children while working to use this model in the healing of trauma within our society. However, while it attempts to limit the ongoing trauma for a child removed from the care of parents, it still does not address the underlying trauma.

The First Thousand Days

The first thousand days of a child's life is a period of rapid development and lays the foundations for the rest of their life. A child's experiences during this period potentially impact health, wellbeing, literacy, economic participation and criminality. We have previously discussed how trauma can influence brain development. However, the brain is not an isolated, standalone organ but is part of a complex, interrelated web. The brain is linked to the body's other systems, including the immune, metabolic and gastrointestinal systems, among others. We are a complex, integrated web of systems that interact with each other and have an impact on each other. This means that the experiences a child has in the first thousand days of life and what we learn during this period not only has an impact on how the brain develops, but on all the other bodily systems the brain is linked to, and this, in turn, can have consequences for the rest of our lives.[94]

The buffering support that parents and other caregivers provide for their children is particularly important during these first two years of life. This is the period where brain architecture is being most actively constructed and it will form the basis for future development. But we don't have to do this alone. Our village, the community we are part of, is central to assisting and supporting parents and children during this period. It is a crucial time in child development and one where the support of those outside the immediate nuclear family unit can help to ensure that the child receives the necessary care and protection. Indigenous and First Nations cultures provide us with a model of the village in action where others in the community have a responsibility for supporting the family and the child. They can step in when the immediate caregivers are not in a position to provide the buffering care needed. Other cultures similarly rely on extended family for support. This is a feature often missing from the dominant Anglo cultures of much of the Western world, where the family unit is often an isolated unit of parents and children. In this environment, the village is, at times, replaced by professional services that provide "drop care" in the form of services such as nursing care, playgroups and early childhood education. In essence, they are paid to care. Although these can provide an essential service, they cannot replace the care of the interconnected community, the tribe.

In Chapters 1 and 2 of this book, we discussed brain development and the impact stress can have on the development of the brain in some detail. One of the important concepts to include with this information on brain development, and closely related to adverse childhood experiences (ACEs), is the importance of the first thousand days of a child's life. This is the period from conception to two years of age. Although the original ACEs Study focused on experiences before the age of 18, we now know that the brain is developing at an incredible pace in the first thousand days of life and that adverse childhood experiences during this time can have a major impact on brain development and potential future outcomes for the child.

This period is when the child is most vulnerable to external influences. While bringing a new life into the world can be something to celebrate, it can also be a time of great stress and change for both parents. Relationships are tested and changed due to the experience of becoming a parent. It is a time when the buffering support of family, friends and community is important so that the stress experienced by the parents and any subsequent behaviour does not have an adverse impact on the developing child.

Brain development begins very early in the pregnancy. By the fourth week of pregnancy, the brain already has approximately 10,000 cells. By the 24th week, this number jumps to 10 billion cells. Stress and any trauma experienced by the mother will produce a hormonal response. The activation of the mother's fight or flight stress response can hinder the child's development. The prenatal period is a vulnerable period for the developing child and one that can have major lifelong impacts, including future brain development, mental health conditions and physical health. It is important during this time that the mother receives appropriate nutrition to support the child's development and that she is under a low level of stress or has buffering support to reduce the impact of stress and trauma on both her and the developing child. If elements of important nutrition are missing, there is a potential for the child to be born with defects. This can include low birth weight, as well as motor and cognitive delays.[95] The risk of future difficulties for the developing child is increased if the mother is under significant stress or has experienced trauma. The additional stresses could include domestic violence, substance abuse, neglect and poverty. These can have a causal relationship to lifelong mental health struggles for the child.[96]

Exposure to toxins such as alcohol and tobacco can also have a lasting impact on the child. There is ample evidence of the effect of alcohol and other substances on the developing foetus. Many would be aware of the warnings to expectant mothers to refrain from using alcohol while they are pregnant.

Exposure of the foetus to alcohol has a major impact on the development of many organs, including the brain. The damage to the brain can result in the underdevelopment of areas of the brain responsible for the control of attention, communication, self-regulation, sensory processing and impulse control. This can mean that the child may have physical and functional difficulties as well as the potential for the development of mental health conditions and behavioural difficulties.[97] This is particularly so if the child's environment is not supportive.

There is also evidence that exposure to tobacco smoke will hurt the child's development if the mother is also going through a stressful pregnancy.[98] If the mother is a member of a family or community suffering the impacts of intergenerational trauma, it can be an even more difficult time for both her and the developing child. These stressors will elevate the level of stress hormones in her system and directly impact the child. Even at this early stage of development, the village is important in how the child develops. This is a time when the parents, and the mother in particular, need the support of the village around her to lower the risk of poor child development. The support and the social contact/connection related to this support can play an important role in reducing the stress experienced by the mother, as well as assist in the healing of any trauma she has experienced.

Humans have evolved to a position where, at birth, many of our systems have already developed so that we can survive in a world outside of the womb. However, some systems are still actively developing. These include the brain, the immune system and the liver. Although the prenatal period is an active period of development at birth, the brain is at the stage where it only functions at the most basic level. The brain at birth can only function enough for the child to survive in the new world it has been brought into. This is the most ancient and primitive part of the brain in action. I've heard this referred to the brain being the "lizard" brain at this stage of development.

The first two years of life see the brain developing incredibly quickly. Developmental growth is most profound during this period. While plasticity will continue for the rest of our lives, there is no other period where the changes are so dynamic. This is the period when the brain is most active and most sensitive to the surrounding environment. This sensitivity can mean that the brain may develop in a maladaptive manner if exposed to adverse events without the buffering support of parents and carers. The extent of maladaptation will be dependent on the neurological stage the brain is at, as well as the intensity, nature and extent of the adverse experience.[99] This maladaptive response can be an important feature in the development of a number of challenges for the developing child, including paediatric disorders such as autism spectrum disorder and attention-deficit hyperactivity disorder (ADHD), among others.

At this point, it will become obvious that it is not a matter of genes vs nature but one of an intricate dance between our genetic makeup and the experiences we have in the periods of dynamic plasticity. It is not a matter of our genetic makeup determining future life outcomes but more the interplay between environment and genes. For instance, a child may be born with a genetic disposition to a medical condition or disorder, but if they do not encounter the experiences that trigger this genetic disposition, the medical condition may not eventuate. While our genes are not altered by the interaction with the world around us, a change is made in how the genes function. The genetic sequence remains the same, but exposure to the environment will result in the gene being expressed or not.[100]

This is sometimes described as being whether the gene is turned on or off. It is referred to as epigenetic change and is most sensitive to being activated during periods of greater brain plasticity and developmental change, such as the first thousand days. Epigenetic change has been identified as a factor in the development of a number of diseases and disorders, such as cardiovascular disease and autism, and can be triggered by the interaction of the gene to particular events and environments.[101] The experiences we have can have a major impact on our lives. Again, this points to the importance of building a village around us to support the child. Buffering our experiences and supporting caregivers is a major function of our community, our village. Without the village, we increase our children's risk of poor outcomes.

Supporting and Buffering the Family

The village plays an important role in supporting and buffering the family. It protects the family from the consequences of potential adverse experiences while reducing and healing the impact of trauma. However, if we don't have the support of the village or the village we have doesn't have the skills and experiences to support and guide us, we may be fortunate enough to have the support of fee-for-service interventions to help in the development of skills to support the child. The great thing is that these services can also help in supporting the village as well as the child. Let's look at how this can work in practice.

Parenting Programs

We've already noted that it is a myth we are born with parenting skills. These are developed through modelling others in action.

Unfortunately, this modelling may not provide a positive outcome for our children as we parent the way we were parented unless we work to change our approach. A parenting program can provide some of the support needed to change our parenting techniques and approaches. Additionally, these programs are often conducted over a period of time. This provides the opportunity for participants to form social connections and begin to build their own village, which can help provide the necessary support previously missing.

Many parenting programs are based on evidence. They have a research base and should provide an informed approach to parenting. However, one major flaw is that many have been developed to serve the dominant cultural group's wishes and are often most successful in supporting white, middle-class, nuclear families. While valuable, there is a real deficit in parenting skill development programs to support other cultures, including Indigenous cultures, that have the ability to reach out to those who would benefit the most from such programs. However, all is not lost. Let's look at two parenting programs bridging the cultural gap and having the potential to be relevant to Indigenous and other culturally diverse communities.

Both of these programs are based in Cairns, Australia. This regional city in far North Queensland has a comparatively high population of people identifying as being Indigenous. At the 2021 Census, 9.8% of the population of Cairns identified as Indigenous. The average for the whole of Australia is 3.2%. The Indigenous population of Cairns represents a significant demographic cohort. A parenting approach having a relevant cultural basis is important in developing the skills of Indigenous parents.

The great thing is that these programs also have relevance to all parents. This is because the programs provide a holistic approach to parenting based on the importance of the village in providing parenting support.

Ngamumu (for Mothers)

In 2022, I had the pleasure of hosting a seminar-breakout room at the Cairns Early Years Conference. This biannual conference attracts keynote speakers, organisations, services and practitioners in the early years sector.

One of the presentations was by Merindi Schrieber and Lia Pa'apa'a. Merindi has a strong cultural connection to Kuku Yalanji (Mossman in Far North Queensland) and is a well-known performer, producer and musician. Lia has a similar strong cultural connection to both Samoan and the Luiseño nation (Southern California). She is an artist, cultural producer and community arts cultural development practitioner. They are both proud First Nations women.

Their presentation was on Ngamumu, a culturally aware parenting program focused on the mother.[102] The program has its base in both the arts and Indigenous cultures. It is designed to support mothers and their babies during the first thousand days of life.

Merindi and Lia developed the program based on their experience during the first thousand days of parenting, where they felt the Western mothering experience lacked the cultural depth and support they sought to sustain them through the important life changes they were experiencing. The program was developed by investigating the common ground within their different cultural backgrounds and then building an arts-based nurturing experience around these common mothering principles. The approach of practitioners in the program is for artists to work with mothers and their babies to re-examine Indigenous cultural practices. This involves discovery of practices for some, and for others, represents a process of rediscovery to incorporate them into their mothering approach. The program provides mothers with an inclusive, safe and cross-generational space to explore the range of cultural supports and practices to bolster and uphold them. Importantly, it also provides a new community of others experiencing the parenting journey who can become part of their village to raise their child.

At the time of the presentation, Ngamumu focused on a ten-week workshop program. This series of workshops explores how the arts and First Nations cultural parenting practices can support mothers. Each series of workshops has a strong cultural basis with an emphasis on the intergenerational exchange of knowledge and the importance of the arts in a cultural approach to child-rearing. Those attending the workshops would participate in cultural activities such as weaving, doll-making, creating lullabies, singing, storytelling and sharing cultural foods as part of the process of parenting and learning.

In many ways, they structured the conference presentation along the same lines as their workshop program, with a healthy dose of culturally relevant arts, crafts and music woven into the information about Ngamumu.

The seminar room was packed with standing room only at the rear. At the conclusion of the presentation, there were requests for the program to expand beyond its geographical location of Far North Queensland.

This is a powerful program and is one of the very few I have seen that explores Indigenous cultural parenting practices that can become part of a contemporary parenting experience. Its power lies in the open acceptance of the generations of cultural knowledge and experience combined with the arts to create an open and accepting parenting program. It brings the knowledge of the tribe and the village back into how each mother can parent their children in a supportive and culturally relevant environment.

Ngamumu provides their parenting workshops face-to-face.

This program is exciting because it has a strong cultural base and combines the power of the arts with cultural elements to provide a meaningful parenting experience for participants. It is also rare in that it looks at the common strengths across a range of First Nations cultural parenting practices and not at the differences in cultural knowledge. This gives the program depth and makes Ngamumu an approach that can be successfully used with mothers who have different cultural understandings and backgrounds. A typical parenting program will rarely start from a First Nations cultural understanding with relevance to people from other cultural experiences. Often, the expectation is that a program based on the contemporary Western nuclear family practice will be relevant to all others regardless of their culture. This sets Ngamumu apart from almost every other parenting approach.

Strengths Men & Fathers

I heard about the Strengths Men & Fathers Program in 2018 while working in community development for a local-government agency. I recall the discussion with Henry and Helen Leafa (the program developers) as if it was yesterday. It was that impressive. Most parenting programs are aimed at mothers or both parents. Strengths Men & Fathers offers a different approach and focuses on the role of men as fathers.

Strengths Men & Fathers is a 6-week program culminating in a fathers and children camp. During the program, a number of important parenting topics for fathers are covered. These are the impact of the father, managing emotions, communication and quality time, emotional intelligence, self-reflection and self-care, fathering well through separation and divorce, ongoing support, and the importance of community. As you can see, the program covers a lot of territory and is really about teaching men how to be fathers. This is just so important. Most of us learn to be fathers from watching our own fathers in the role. For many, this has not been a positive experience, especially in those families where the father was often away working or was a distant parent. The Strengths Men & Fathers Program conveys important parenting skills but also aims to lift the father's self-esteem, provide him with skills to better deal with his emotions, and invite him to be more vulnerable and available to his children and others in his community.

The success of the program is shown in the source of the majority of its referrals. Many other programs receive the bulk of their referrals from other programs and services. However, Strengths Men & Fathers receives the majority of its referrals through those fathers who have previously completed the program. Often, the referral is to friends or work colleagues.

Strengths Men & Fathers has been in operation for almost 10 years and has assisted over 1,000 men in re-evaluating how they parent and changing their approach to their families and their children. Strengths Men & Fathers is a program open to men of all ages and cultural backgrounds, and it welcomes foster parents, grandparents and step-parents (i.e., anyone in a fathering role).

It shows its cultural relevance in that men from all cultural backgrounds have felt welcome and have completed the program. They have changed their parenting to reflect the new knowledge and skills they have learnt in the course of the workshops.

One of the positive features of the program is that former participants are invited back at some point during the program to share with the new attendees how the program has made a difference to them and how it has changed their relationship with their children.

Its success has a strong foundation of skill development and it reinforces the importance of building a community around the father and creating the village to raise the child.

In conducting the program, Henry has found the biggest problem for men is loneliness. When problems arise, many men feel they have no one to talk to, and then they bottle up their feelings until they can no longer contain them, resulting in violence, abuse and neglect.[103]

While Henry and Helen Leafa coordinate the program, other fathers are involved in facilitating the workshops. This assists in conveying the important messages as they are coming not just from one person. The same messages are being transmitted by others involved in the program.

A highlight of the program is the final fathers and children camp. This is an activity-rich experience that involves camping, rock climbing, problem solving, caving and cooking. This camp is designed to cement the bond between the father and his children.

A bonus is that the program is offered free of charge. All costs are covered by funding made available by the federal government through the Communities for Children program. This program operates in over 50 locations throughout Australia. It targets areas classified as suffering social and economic disadvantage. Funds are locally allocated to programs providing targeted services for children aged 0–12, but they can also include young people up to 18.

Playgroups

Parenting can be a difficult and isolating experience for many. This is particularly so in the early years of a child's life before they commence school. As babies and young children are vulnerable, they require the ongoing and available support of a loving caregiver to flourish. Without this buffering support, the child is at risk of suffering toxic stress and trauma, resulting in potentially negative life outcomes. It is a time of change for both parents and can place great stress on families.

It is a period when at least one parent is at home with the child most of the time. For many parents, this results in them shutting themselves off from their social connections and networks at a time when they require the support of family, friends and community. Again, this highlights one of the flaws in the Western model of isolated nuclear families carrying the responsibility for parenting. The support of the village is essential in providing support, respite, alternative parenting and care for the child and the parents.

Without an extended family or community to support the parents, other options are fortunately available, often in the form of services. Many of these are fee-for-service arrangements and can represent a high-cost barrier to some parents needing the most support. These types of services include kindergartens and long day care. These early childhood learning services allow the parent to return to employment and other endeavours while the child still receives an early learning experience. These early learning experiences help to prepare the child for entry into school. An alternative to these programs is a playgroup.

Playgroups are environments where the parent stays with the child during the period the group is operating. They bring several parents and families together, allowing children to meet and play with other children while also allowing the parent to meet other parents, share concerns, build relationships and establish new networks. Playgroups meet regularly, often weekly, and are open to children 0–5 years of age. Playgroups aim to assist children in building bonds with other children.

This assists in their childhood development. The playgroup environment also allows parents to meet with other parents, carers and professionally trained early childhood educators at some playgroups.

Playgroups assist parents in learning new skills, sharing their experiences and ideas with other parents, and building new parenting and caring skills through developing greater confidence in raising their families. An additional and crucial aspect of playgroups is the building of community and social connections between parents. For some, this can be the greatest aspect of the playgroup. They get to know other parents in a similar situation and build social networks they can expand on outside of the playgroup experience.

Playgroups are offered either by community-based parent groups or often through professional early childhood education agencies. One community-based charity providing support for families and parents in Australia is Play Matters. This began as a group of mothers in Mt Gravatt in Queensland who wanted to establish playgroups for their children. In 1973, these parents established the Playgroup Association of Queensland as a not-for-profit, non-religious organisation run by volunteers. At the time, options for early childhood education were limited, with the only option to establish your own group to provide the support required. By 1974, the organisation had 120 affiliated playgroups. Play Matters is now one of Australia's largest community-based charities providing support for families and parents.

Healthy Eating Playgroup

The Healthy Eating Playgroup is offered by Play Matters to parents and children in Cairns, Queensland. The playgroup is supported financially by the Communities for Children Program. This means there is no fee attached to the program.

The playgroup was established in response to a request from one of the parents. Some attending playgroups in the area are parents who have relocated to Australia from Asian countries. Some of these parents have partners who have moved to Australia for employment, while others are married to or partnered with an Australian-born parent. Many of these parents are not only isolated from their surrounding community, but also culturally isolated.

The initial request was from a mother who wanted to prepare meals for her children using foods readily available in the local supermarkets. She had found the range of foods in Australian supermarkets very different from those in her home country. She wanted to know how to make low- cost and healthy meals for her family using locally available ingredients. She also wanted her children to have food available in their lunchboxes that didn't make them feel out of place with other children when they went to school.

The team at Play Matters developed the Healthy Eating Playgroup program for those parents who were interested. Numbers are limited at this playgroup. The original design was for the playgroup to be conducted over 10 weeks of a school term with a different cohort of parents and children attending the program the following term. However, many parents return to the playgroup during the next term.

The design for the playgroup is that the parents prepare food for their children's lunch. Each week's meal is planned in advance, with Play Matters staff selecting cheap food supplies. Sometimes, this will include meat, but it always includes a range of locally available vegetables. The aim is for the meals to be healthy and available at a low cost.

For most sessions, the parents prepare meals for their children, but there is at least one session where the children prepare a meal for their parents. This is usually a simple snack. However, this provides the children with exposure to food preparation and assists in building a closer bond between the parent and the child.

In observing this playgroup for over a year, I have noticed that the parents have built a firm bond with each other and will often meet for coffee or some other socialising opportunity outside of the timeframe of the playgroup. This has helped build a supportive community that may have been previously missing from these parents' lives. They have created their own village of mutual support. As many come from similar cultural backgrounds, it has also resulted in the parents feeling less culturally isolated and increased their confidence as both parents and contributing members of their local communities.

The playgroup is facilitated by Play Matters staff members, Di and Amanda. They have worked hard to make it the success it has become over the past two years. Each week during school term, they arrive at the venue early to set up tables, chairs and toys for the children. They then set up the cooking utensils in the venue's function room where they are meeting. Before the day, they prepare a menu, purchase ingredients and make any necessary substitutions. They aim to make healthy meals on a tight budget. Often, the meals they prepare are vegetarian. Di told me recently, "It's amazing how a can of lentils can substitute for meat or bulk up a meal."

During the playgroup, Di and Amanda move between the parents cooking and the children playing. A walk through the cooking area is guaranteed to bring on hunger spasms. It is really encouraging to hear the parents talking and laughing together.

Recently, I asked one of the parents if they were afraid they would stop cooking their traditional meals. More than one participant chimed in with a loud "no". Although they have started cooking Western meals at home, they continue to prepare traditional meals and food as well.

A simple request to learn how to make food using local ingredients has grown into an established and connected community for those attending the playgroup. Although originally aimed at parents from culturally and linguistically diverse (CALD) backgrounds, I have noticed an increased number of parents attending from the general community who do not feel culturally displaced. It is encouraging to see a multicultural and diverse community growing from this simple idea for a playgroup. The Healthy Eating Playgroup shows the creation of a supportive village in a microcosm. It is through these simple social connections, where we extend the nuclear family to include other parents, children and friends, that we build the village to support the child and also enhance the lives of the parents. It is as simple as meeting together. The presence of food as an attractor to this playgroup has no doubt been important in building the sense of community participants' experience. After all, it is over the breaking of bread that we often most easily connect with each other.

A related Play Matters project, also facilitated by Amanda and Di, is a community garden at a local state primary school. Again, Play Matters received funding from the Communities for Children Program to restore the garden to use it as part of Play Matters programs at the school. This was very much a partnership between the school, Play Matters and the Communities for Children program.

The garden had fallen into disrepair and hadn't been used by the school for some time. Play Matters wanted to rebuild the garden to use with playgroups, particularly the playgroup running at the school on Monday mornings of the school term. I had seen photographs of the garden before Play Matters commenced work on it. It was overgrown with weeds and very rundown. Over a six-month period, the garden had been cleaned up and Di had been working to replant and lovingly tend it. I visited the playgroup one August morning. In Australia, this is towards the end of winter. In Cairns, this is partway through the dry season. This is the prime growing time for vegetables in Far North Queensland. The garden was neat. Several raised beds had been planted out and the plants were thriving. There were herbs, tomatoes, passionfruit and strawberries all growing well. Di was preparing it for the morning playgroup. The morning's activities involved children and parents in planting, watering and tending to the plants. This provides an excellent opportunity for bonding between parents and children as well as teaching them how to successfully grow food crops in the local environment. Di and Amanda will spend time with the participants discussing how to grow the plants successfully at home, ideas for small gardens and how the various fruits, herbs and vegetables can be used. This is a real achievement with the potential for the garden to provide a learning experience and an opportunity to further build the village that can provide a nurturing environment for local children.

Poverty, Trauma and the Village

As a society, we do ourselves, our families and our children immeasurable harm by not addressing intergenerational and childhood trauma. We are sowing the seeds for future family, social and criminal problems. We are wealthy, developed nations in the West with the means to address childhood trauma but we lack the political and social will to make the tough decisions. Failing to address trauma guarantees that social problems will continue to grow and impact the next generation of our children. Poverty is one of the simplest problems to solve that would have a major impact on future generations. We have the financial resources to address poverty in our societies at its root. Still, we are often held back because those with the greatest resources are unwilling to surrender any portion of their wealth to address the issue of poverty, one of the drivers of trauma.

The majority of wealth in Western nations is held in the hands of the privileged few, and many will pass this wealth on to their children. Although they are not immune from trauma, they are protected from one of its drivers—poverty. Some of this reluctance to share their bounty is flawed beliefs about those trapped in poverty. Often, being poor is not the fault of the person suffering from the consequences of poverty. They are trapped in a cycle of surviving on the available meagre funds. At the same time, we have the solution at our fingertips but are largely unwilling to take necessary action.

Without the social and political will to redistribute wealth so that none are left behind in poverty, it is up to the village to support those in greatest need by connecting and mobilising the assets they have to create change. Perhaps the most important thing the village can do is to offer the support to all that is found in the Indigenous and First Nations models, where all village members share responsibility for the wellbeing of the child and the reduction of preventable trauma.

CHAPTER 12:

Community and Wellbeing

In Chapter 5, we discussed the functions of a connected community. One of those functions was enabling health. We looked briefly at this function, but let's now look at it a little deeper.

In May 2023, the United States Surgeon General released *Our Epidemic of Loneliness and Isolation: The U.S. Surgeon General's Advisory on the Healing Effects of Social Connection and Community*.[104] The Surgeon General releases publications about issues they believe have an important impact on the health and wellbeing of the citizens of the United States. In this document, they have outlined the depth of the problem of loneliness and isolation, how it impacts our health and what we can do about it. This is an important document. As such, I will refer to it throughout much of this chapter. Reference will also be made to the *Australian Loneliness Report*.[105] This report is based on the findings of a national survey of Australian adults and their wellbeing. The survey was conducted between 29 May 2018 and 1 October 2018.

Isolation and loneliness are two separate but often interrelated conditions. Isolation is an objective state of having limited relationships with other people, limited social roles and a lack of membership of social groups. It can be characterised by limited social interaction. Loneliness is a much more subjective state. It is an internal experience based on perceptions of isolation and feeling that your social experience does not match up to your expectations.[106] It is not about the number of friendships and relationships a person has, but rather the quality of these relationships.

When we start to feel lonely, it is a sign we need to find a way to connect with others in a way that we can feel valued. From this comes that important sense of belonging.

Isolation and loneliness can not only influence our sense of wellbeing but have a major impact on our health and longevity. Loneliness can increase the risk of premature death by 26%, and isolation can increase this risk by 29%. This has, at times, been compared to the risk of smoking 15 cigarettes a day.

Healthwise, a lack of (or poor) community connection is one of the underlying conditions increasing the risk of heart disease by 29%, and stroke by 32%. It is also a component of increasing the risk for the development of anxiety disorders, depressive conditions and dementia, as well as impacting our immune system, making us more likely to have low resistance to viruses and other respiratory illnesses.[107]

Historically, we needed to be socially connected to survive. In times past, we relied on one another for our safety and protection. This has left us as a species with a need to be connected. It could be said we are hardwired to seek out connection with others. Even in the age of social media and the online ordering of goods and services, including food, we are still driven to connect more meaningfully with others. It is not our natural state to live with loneliness or in isolation. Yet when surveyed, only 39% of adults in the United States could say they felt very connected with other people, and almost half of the population of adults are experiencing a state of loneliness.[108]

A similar situation was found in Australia, with one in four adults surveyed stating they were lonely. Over half the population (50.5%) indicated they felt lonely for at least one day per week, while 27.6% identified as being lonely for three or more days each week.[109] This represents a major problem as a high level of social connection leads to positive health outcomes, while lower levels of connection lead to poorer outcomes.

This lack of individual social connection is reflected in our broader society and revealed in lower trust levels. For example, in 1972, 45% of American citizens stated that they trusted others, but by 2016, this had dropped to 30%.[110] The same decline in trust is regularly shown in polls relating to the trust people have in politicians and the operating political systems. With lower social connection, trust is one of the first major casualties.

Various studies and research show that we spend more time alone now than we have in the past. In 2003, Americans spent an average of 142.5 hours alone each month. By 2020, this had increased to 166.5 hours a month. We are also spending less time with friends in person. In 2003, American adults spent 30 hours each month socialising with friends. By 2020, this had reduced to 10 hours each month. For young people aged 15–24, the time spent socialising with their peers dropped from 150 minutes per day in 2003 to 40 minutes per day in 2020.[111]

At the same time, the number of people we consider to be close friends has declined. In 1990, 27% of those surveyed said they had three or fewer close friends. By 2021, this had increased to 49% of the population.[112] Again, this decline in friendships is reflected in other Western nations. As mentioned earlier in this book, Australian adults had an average of nine friends they could trust and rely on in 1984. By 2023, this had reduced to five.[113] It's quite startling how only over a few decades the level of social connection (community) has declined in our societies.

One of the most obvious impacts of this decline is that we have fewer people we can rely on in times of need and few supports to help us heal from trauma.

We are also observing a decline in community participation. For example, fewer people identify as attending a church or other place of worship. While in itself this may simply mean the community is becoming more secular, religious participation has not been replaced with other social participation. Along with attending a place of worship often comes involvement in other church-related groups and provides ready-made support when needed. Along with a decline in religious affiliation, there are declines in trade union membership, other group membership and club membership. Again, these have not been replaced with other group connections. And in 2018 only 16% of Americans felt connected to their local community.[114]

Community Connection and Health Outcomes

There is a correlation between social connection and good health. Generally, a high level of social connection will result in positive health outcomes. Social connection is also important in other areas. There are links between social connection, workplace satisfaction, income and general wellbeing. A lack of social connection is a higher-risk factor than other health indicators, such as smoking 15 cigarettes a day, drinking 6 or more alcoholic beverages a day, physical inactivity, obesity and air pollution, among others.[115] It is just that important.

Let's look at some of these health outcomes a little closer:

- **Longevity.** Research from a number of different scientific approaches shows that people who live in a connected community have a high chance of living longer. Estimates of the worth of social connection indicate that those who have a close community around them increase their chance of longevity by 50%. However, those living isolated lives, suffering from loneliness or having poverty in their relationships have a much higher chance of dying younger, regardless of the cause of death. The degree to which a person lives in close connection with others is comparable and perhaps more important in their health outcomes than other factors.

- **Cardiovascular disease and strokes.** A lack of social relationships or poor social connection can increase the chance of a person having a heart attack by 29% and a stroke by 32%. Isolation or other trauma experienced in childhood increases the adult risk factors for both conditions. These risk factors include obesity, high blood pressure and high blood glucose levels. The evidence is so overwhelming that the American Heart Foundation in 2022 said: "Social isolation and loneliness are common, yet underrecognised, determinants of cardiovascular health and brain health."[116] Those who already have heart failure and have high levels of loneliness increased their risk of hospitalisation by 68%, emergency department visits by 57%, and had a 26% increased risk of outpatient visits than those with low levels of loneliness. Researchers also found that poor social connection is associated with a 55% higher chance of hospital readmission. Those living in a connected community and/or who had others living with them had a greater chance of receiving treatment than those with low levels of social connection. This is due to the support provided by connections in the event of heart failure. This social connection increases the chance of survival from a heart attack.
- **Hypertension—high blood pressure.** Again, the research shows that those with greater social connections

have a lower risk of developing high blood pressure even if they are in a high-risk category for hypertension. Social interaction can aid in reducing the effects of hypertension once it has been diagnosed.

- **Type 2 diabetes.** Those with greater social and emotional support have a lower risk of developing type 2 diabetes than those with poor social support. Again, like hypertension, once diagnosed and treated, the ongoing maintenance of the disease is better for those living in a connected community than those with poor social connection. It seems much can be said for the support of others in us maintaining our treatment regime and working to live healthier lives.

- **Immune system.** In earlier chapters, we discussed the impact of adverse childhood experiences (ACEs) on the developing immune system. Those experiencing a high level or occurrence of toxic stress have a higher risk of compromising their immune system and are likely to have lower immunity to disease throughout their lives. Additionally, those disconnected from their community or suffering loneliness with poor social support have a greater chance of developing severe diseases once exposed to viruses such as the common cold than those with greater social connection and support. There is even evidence that poor social connection contributes to how we respond to vaccination. An example of this is COVID-19 vaccinations. The research found that those with a poor social connection to their neighbours and who were lonely had a weaker antibody response to the vaccine, lowering its effectiveness.

- **Cognitive functioning.** Those living isolated lives and who are lonely have a 50% higher risk of developing dementia as they age than those living socially connected lives. Further research shows that isolation from social contact and loneliness can result in our cognitive functioning deteriorating 20% faster than those with positive social connections. The evidence clearly shows that building a strong local community, spending time with family and friends, and enjoying social engagements is one of the key strategies in delaying or preventing the onset of dementia.

- **Mental health conditions.** Loneliness and isolation increase the risk of developing anxiety disorders and depressive conditions. This is made worse by a characteristic of anxiety and depression that entices people to withdraw socially from others. Those who regularly feel lonely are at twice the risk of developing these conditions than someone having positive social experiences with other people. The *Australian Loneliness Survey* found that loneliness increased the risk of experiencing depression by 15.2% and social anxiety by 13.1%. It also found that depression increased the risk of experiencing loneliness by 10.6% and social anxiety by 8.6%.[117] It is a self-reinforcing circle.

- **Suicide and self-harm.** A high level of connection to others is a protective factor in suicide and self-harm. For men with poor social connections and living alone, the risk of suicide is much higher than those with good social connections. The US Surgeon General has theorised that this may be because those contemplating suicide have a low sense of belonging and believe they are a burden to others. It has also been shown there is a close link between a sense of loneliness and a lack of social support as a primary contributing factor to incidents of self-harm. In short, being socially connected to others is a strong protective factor in both suicide and self-harm.[118]

How Does Being Part of a Connected Community Affect Health and Wellbeing Outcomes?

We've spoken about the impact of social connection on our health, but exactly how does this work? How does being in a connected community affect our health? The evidence is pretty clear that it strongly influences our health, so let's look at how it works.

Like most things in our lives, the relationship between health outcomes and community involves a network of associations. We will look at the following three processes: biological, psychological and behavioural.

Biological

We have already examined the connection between the buffering support of a caregiver in the first thousand days of life and the developing brain. In simple terms, the support of a parent or other caregiver in highly stressful times can buffer the impact of toxic stress on the developing brain. This support can help mitigate the activation of stress hormones, which can significantly impact how our brains develop. Activating these hormones for elevated periods will then further impact the development of some of our bodily organs. Likewise, social connections can influence our biological networks throughout our lives.

Our biological systems do not operate independently of one another. A change in one of these systems can create a change in others. For example, there is a connection between social isolation, loneliness and inflammation in the body. Inflammation, in turn, is a contributing factor to many diseases and adverse health conditions, such as heart disease, cancer, diabetes, depression and Alzheimer's. It is also linked to early mortality. Feeling socially isolated and having few social supports can have the same impact on the body as being physically inactive and

158

it can increase inflammation throughout the body. Conversely, having positive social support in place and being in a connected community can have positive impacts on biological systems and health conditions. It has the potential to improve cardiovascular functioning, blood pressure and the neuroendocrine system.[119]

Psychological

Social connectedness has an impact on our psychological processes. As a species, we are a social beast. We need to be in connection with others. Many of us will readily admit that being in a positive relationship with our family, friends and others creates a sense of wellbeing and provides a buffer during hard times. Often, we gain a sense of meaning and purpose from our social connections.

Without them, we can easily start to feel lost and drift into isolation. Having a sense of meaning and purpose contributes to us being able to pursue meaningful life goals that can include taking action to pursue positive health outcomes.

Positive social supports will provide a buffer when difficult times come our way and reduce the stress in these situations. This is because we have others to turn to in seeking support and feel capable of contacting professional services when required. Without these supports, toxic stress can impact our health outcomes. Research also indicates a strong link between stress and obesity, mental illness and diabetes.

Let's look at an example of this in action. On 31 July 2023, Eleanor de Jong wrote about the power of the community in recovering from a mental health incident.[120]

In her short article, she detailed her experience recovering from mental health episodes. She discusses the pressure placed on her immediate family and friends. She feels they bear her trauma. They are the ones hiding the knives, ensuring her medication is taken, ensuring substance abuse is minimised and they are often the people who need to call for medical assistance or even the police in a time of crisis. One of the points she raises is our focus on the nuclear family. There can be times we fail to look further than this social unit when we need support (i.e., we need to remember the power of the actions of our community in our healing and not just our immediate family). De Jong mentions the support of a university lecturer who permitted her to sit in on a literature class for a term even though she wasn't enrolled. This enabled her to focus on other things besides her health condition and struggle. Or the neighbour who invited her out to coffee once or twice a week, even though they rarely spoke, so he played her the piano instead of talking a great deal. Then there is the ex-boy-friend who visited her in the hospital or the brother's girlfriend that she doesn't even know who baked her a cake. These are the tiny supports that help us deal with our trauma through their brief interventions and they help us to heal. They are experiences where we are accepted for who we are, not what is hurting us, and they lift us so we can pause and have a break from our problems. We are then better equipped to move forward to deal with the struggles that life throws our way.[121]

Behavioural

Being connected to others has a direct impact on the behaviours we adopt and the choices we make. These choices will include lifestyle factors such as diet, exercise and sleep, as well as maintaining treatment plans, taking medications and making positive health choices. This positive relationship with others will mean they can provide support and encouragement for us to maintain our health regime, take our medication and make better health choices. For example, a while back, I was having a conversation with a work colleague. We had both taken up running to improve our health outcomes. She told me about the features of a particular running watch she found helpful in retaining a focus on her running goals. I purchased this watch and found it to be all she said it was. Just wearing it reminded me of the physical exercise I needed to undertake that day to achieve my goals.[122]

A Bigger Picture

So far in this chapter, we have discussed the importance of a connected community and social support for the individual. However, the benefits of living in close social connection with others has a broader impact than just on the individual. It has a benefit for the whole community. Let's now briefly examine some of these benefits.

The Health of the Community

In simple terms, communities with a high level of social connection are concerned with the good of the whole society, not just the individual. They work for the common good. Places with a high level of social connection also have higher levels of social capital than communities with low levels of connection. Social capital is a by-product of connection. This increase in social capital will often result in better health outcomes across the community due to the acts of individuals to ensure that the common good is maintained. Many studies are showing this relationship. Those communities with increased levels of social capital have lower mortality rates, a greater rate of survival from medical episodes, higher self-reporting of good health and lower rates of readmissions to hospitals than communities with lower levels of social capital.

People living in communities with higher rates of social connection are also more likely to seek medical assistance when needed and to adopt positive health behaviours such as a higher vaccine uptake rate. These behaviours have a ripple effect throughout the whole community, not just for the individual, as they reduce the potential for spreading disease.

The opposite is true for communities with lower social capital and community connection. The COVID-19 pandemic provided an example of this in operation. Those areas with higher levels of social capital experienced fewer deaths and lower infection rates than those with lower social capital. This may be related to socially connected population cohorts exhibiting a higher level of trust in government advice and, therefore, greater adherence to safe behaviours, the maintenance of recommended vaccination regimes, and a desire to act to benefit others and not only themselves.[123]

Natural Disasters

We will examine this in greater detail in the next chapter; however, how a community responds and recovers to a natural disaster such as fire, flood, earthquake or cyclone has a relationship to how connected the community is and the level of social capital displayed by that community. In short, a connected community will display a greater willingness to prepare for imminent disasters, be more willing to follow official advice, and more prepared to share information and resources with others. All this leads to a quicker immediate response by residents, greater cooperation when the disaster hits, and a greater chance of working together to recover compared to those with poorer social connection.

I recall attending a conference and hearing Phil Koperberg speak about the importance of a connected community during a bushfire. At the time, he was the NSW Rural Fire Service

162

Commissioner. His role meant that he was often away from home during disasters, working in control centres to operate bushfire response units, and advising the government and media of progress. He spoke of the time a major bushfire impacted his town. He received a call from his neighbour saying the fire was getting closer and asking Phil if he wanted him to hose down the roof, ensuring it was wet and giving it greater protection from the fire. Of course, he gave his neighbour permission. His house was saved, as were all the houses in his street, but houses a few streets over were burnt out. There were elderly residents in those streets out who had never met their neighbours, and protective actions such as those undertaken by Phil's neighbour were not undertaken. Phil went on to say that the connection between his own neighbours made the difference.[124]

Community Safety

We have already examined the benefits of social connection and safe places. In general, those places with a strong sense of community are safer and have lower rates of violence and lower rates of crimes such as car theft.

Local Economy

Communities with high levels of social connection will usually have more resilient economies. They tend to be places where people readily share information regarding employment and business opportunities, they are less impacted by economic downturns, are places where people work together on new ideas, and are centres of innovation. There is also a strong investment in the local economy due to a concern that investing in local businesses benefits their community and not some far-off corporation.

Motivated Citizens

Connected communities investing in local businesses are communities activated for change. They are places where people work together to create change. They have a great deal in common and identify issues that are important enough for them to take action. They form volunteer groups to maintain local parks, start community gardens, raise petitions and see themselves as agents of change, not the recipients of service from the government and other agencies.

These communities are places where people take their civic role seriously and actively engage in the political process. They lobby their elected representatives, vote, and sometimes take political action to build a better place where they live.

Building the Community

In this chapter, we've spoken about the importance of social connection and being part of a community in terms of creating health and wellbeing. In Chapter 7, we looked at a number of approaches to this. Now, let's look briefly at some very simple actions you can do to get started in building your own local community.

Neighbour Day

If you haven't tried getting to know your neighbours, it can feel intimidating. If you feel this way, it might be easy to tie your attempt to something special. A great example of this is Neighbour Day. This is celebrated in Australia on the last Sunday of every March. But every day can be Neighbour Day.

The first Neighbour Day was held in March 2003 and was branded as a time "to check on your neighbours". Andrew Heslop founded the day after hearing a story in his local community about how an older adult had been found deceased in their house. They had passed away sometime before, but the person had no one who could check up on their wellbeing and welfare. The concept was simple: plan a small activity to get to know your neighbours. Since that first Neighbour Day, it has been celebrated every year in March.

In 2014, Relationships Australia took on responsibility for being the facilitating body for Neighbour Day. Relationships Australia is an organisation working to build respectful relationships between people. They have rebranded the event as Neighbours Every Day. This means it is now a year-round opportunity to undertake actions to get to know your neighbours. The official Neighbour Day in March is now a dedicated day of action. Neighbours Every Day is a campaign centred around social connection to end loneliness across Australia. With it being a year-long campaign, there is no reason why you can't start today and host your first activity to get to know your neighbours.

Relationships Australia have conducted extensive research into the impact of the campaign. They have found that people show a greater identification with the neighbourhood they live in following the event. And that both those who host an activity and those who attend an activity show greater identification with their neighbourhood than those who don't attend. They have also found that those involved in Neighbours Every Day activities experienced a greater sense of wellbeing during COVID-19 pandemic lockdowns, had improved mental health outcomes, reported a reduced sense of loneliness and experienced less psychological distress.

They also found a strong flow-on effect from Neighbours Every Day in the quality of relationships between people. This effect was not just between neighbours but also included family, friends, extended family, colleagues and former colleagues. People extended their social networks and were more interested in socialising after attending a Neighbours Every Day activity.[125]

The Neighbours Every Day website has extensive resources to assist in getting to know your neighbours. There are connection cards to introduce yourself to your neighbours, calling cards, templates for invitations, tips for planning and holding activities, and many more resources and ideas. Why not start today by visiting their website and starting to get to know your neighbours?[126]

Neighbour Happy Hour

Organising a get-together with your neighbours is something that is very easy to do. Choose a time, date and location for the get-together. This could be your front or backyard, driveway, verge/nature strip at the front of your house or a local park. Design and print invitations on your computer and distribute them to your neighbours. If you are nervous or shy, put the invitations into the neighbours' letterboxes. However, you will have more people attending your get-together if you knock on their door and talk to them. This is a more personal approach and makes it easy on the day as those attending will already have met you.

You can cater for the event yourself or ask people to bring something to share. The simpler the planning, the better. Sometimes, planning an activity for the get-together will help break the ice for people who may not have seen each other before. To simplify it, it's a good idea to tie your get-together to a special celebration. This could be Christmas, New Year, Halloween or some other celebration throughout the year. Having it as part of a time of the year that people already associate with a period of celebration will give them a good reason to attend and have some fun.

The simplest idea I've seen for street get-togethers like this is the "neighbour happy hour". People already associate a happy hour with winding down after work. So, a happy hour for the neighbours could attract them. The great thing about a neighbour happy hour is that it is easy to organise. A hand-drawn flyer that is photocopied and placed in letterboxes is the easiest way to promote one. Tell people to bring their own drinks, snacks and chairs on your flyer. You can host it in your driveway or verge in front of your house. An added plus about the happy hour is that it is a time-limited activity, e.g., 4 p.m.–6 p.m. This makes it easier for people to schedule attending the event and not feel overburdened by it. Happy hours work best if they are a regular event so that after a while, people know that it will be on. It is such a simple idea that it can move from house to house so that one neighbour feels overly responsible for organising the event.

Sarah Paints Rocks

Sarah lives on a busy street and wanted to get to know her neighbours. A local organisation had been promoting street get-togethers as a way to get to know neighbours. As part of this promotion, they offered to help by providing a template for an invitation and advice on planning the event, as well as printing the flyers and attending on the day to help. Sarah took up the offer of the get-together with her neighbours. She decided to organise it in a local park.

On the day, only a few neighbours turned up. Most who turned up were retired and felt isolated. One even walked past the get-together two or three times before they dared to join in.

Although she was a little disappointed at the low turnout, she decided to try again. This time, she planned the get-together on the verge at the front of her house. She invited all her neighbours, but this time, Sarah door-knocked each neighbour's house to invite them. This provided her with the opportunity to meet people before the event. For the day, she had planned an activity of painting rocks. This is an activity Sarah had been doing by herself for some time. It is a very simple, creative and fun activity. It involves collecting smooth creek stones, painting a picture or design on the them and then applying lacquer. She had seen this at other events where painted rocks were distributed throughout a venue for children to find. With Sarah's street get-together, whoever painted the rock could take it home with them once the paint was dry. This time, she attracted more of her neighbours, and people engaged in lively discussions with each other. She is certain this is partly due to her introducing herself to her neighbours through door-knocking.

The combination of a planned activity, promoting the rock painting as something the whole family could do, and having the event in the street itself also helped to attract people.

CHAPTER 13:

Natural Disasters

One is Left

Fire swept across the ridge
And then up the mountainside
Flames were fanned by roaring winds
And the smoke blacked out the sky
They thought at first they were gone
Losing everything they had
Fire is a deadly beast
It has no respect for man

Chorus:
One is gone and one remains
And there's nothing left to show
One a blessing one a curse
That's the way the story goes

Told them then that they should go
And leave everything behind
Flames are getting closer now
Got to go there is no time
It's a race against the fire
Time to cry and say goodbye

Turn around for one last look
If you stayed you'd surely die

Fire reached their street at night
There was nothing could be done
Flames are stretching to the roof
Burning hotter than the sun
Takes one house but leaves the next
Fire is the devil's seed
Has no thought for what it does
Takes everything then it leaves

— Alan Blackshaw 2005

Collective Trauma

Just as individuals can suffer trauma, so can groups of people and communities. It can come from several events and incidents but is powerful enough to leave a scar on the whole community. It can come from economic trauma, such as when a major business closes or an employer leaves the area. It can come from mining accidents or bus crashes, and it can come from natural disasters. These events can have a major traumatic impact on a community; sometimes, it is not just one event. For example, a community may be hit by a natural disaster such as a fire and then lose major employers from the area, compounding the trauma felt. In this section, we will focus on the trauma of natural disasters, but, in general, the discussion will relate to other collective traumas that result after major events.

The 2003 Canberra Bushfires

A natural disaster can happen at any time. Some of them come with very little warning; others may provide us with some warning. There are tsunamis, floods, fires, extreme temperatures, tornados, hurricanes, and where I live, cyclones. Natural disasters are traumatic and can leave a scar that can take years to heal. Once again, it is the community where most of this healing occurs. As I sit and write this chapter, extreme temperatures are devastating many European countries. In Greece, there are unprecedented fires, and in Death Valley in the USA, the highest temperatures ever seen are being recorded. The frequency and ferocity of natural disasters are increasing due to climate change, which we have collectively failed to address adequately.

In 2002, Australia suffered one of its most severe droughts on record. During that year, Canberra, Australia's capital, received very little rainfall and experienced low humidity and very high temperatures. These are high-risk conditions for bushfires.

On 8 January 2003, a lightning strike ignited three fires in the Namadgi National Park and one in the Brindabella National Park. Attempts to control the fires were unsuccessful and they spread out of control. Eventually, the four fires merged, posing a potential threat to Canberra, particularly in some outlying suburbs.

On 17 January, weather conditions were poor. There were strong winds, high temperatures and low humidity. These conditions made the fire worse. Firefighters were withdrawn from trying to contain the fires and directed to protect property to minimise damage and protect the lives of those in the path of the fire.

On 18 January, the fires spread to the outlying suburbs of Canberra. At 2:40 p.m., the first public emergency message was broadcast, and at 2:45 p.m., the Australian Capital Territory's Chief Minister declared a state of emergency. During the afternoon, power and communications were blacked out by the fire. Many residents left their homes to escape the fire. Some stayed on to protect their property. The Canberra Hospital was crowded with people suffering from smoke inhalation and burns.

Conditions eased that night and the fires were under control by the next day.

Four people died in these fires and 435 were injured. Approximately 70% of the Australian Capital Territory was burned. 487 homes and 23 government and commercial buildings were destroyed, including the Mount Stromlo Observatory. The estimated financial cost was between $600 million to $1 billion.[127] But that doesn't take into account the personal loss to people and the resulting trauma. A photograph I saw of the Parliament House in Canberra taken during daylight hours, at the height of the fires, looked like it was in the middle of the night.

On 18 January, my sister and her family attended a family get-together two hours away from her home in Canberra. During the family function, she received a call from one of her neighbours who told her how bad the fires had become and that he would hose down the roof of her house to extinguish any glowing embers from the fires that might land on her house. Often, houses catch fire at some distance from the fire itself due to these embers landing on them and igniting. The actions of her neighbour potentially protected her property. If she did not know her neighbour, it is highly likely that this protective action would not have occurred.

I wrote *One is Left*, the song lyrics at the opening of this chapter, as a reflection on the 2003 Canberra bushfires.

The 2022 Lismore Floods

The first responders to any natural disaster are unlikely to be professionals such as firefighters, police or rescue services. They are likely to be neighbours and members of the local community who are already at the scene. Part of our human hardwiring is to protect our tribe. We protect those around us when a disaster occurs to ensure our tribe survives. This is an ancient part of our development that's buried in our brain.

In early 2022, Lismore in Northern NSW was impacted by the most severe floods ever recorded in Australia. In the days leading up to the floods, the region experienced three major periods of rain. Individually, each one of these storms would have been enough to cause a moderate flood, but when they occurred very close to each other, the result was devastating. Both the Bureau of Meteorology and the State Emergency Service were caught off-guard, with neither of these agencies issuing a warning about the potential flooding. In response to the rising flood waters, people did what they normally did if a flood was imminent. They moved vehicles to higher ground and valuables to an upper level in their homes. But this flood was 2 metres higher than any previous flood. At their peak, the flood waters were recorded at 14.4 metres. Buildings that had never flooded before were inundated with water. People were trapped in their homes. Over 31,000 people were impacted across the Lismore local government area.

Things can change rapidly in a natural disaster such as a flood or a fire. This was the case for Lismore. On 26 February, 2022, at 11:37 am, residents received a warning for minor flooding of the Wilson River. During the day, flood waters reached a maximum of 3.8 metres and Lismore received 4 mm of rain. Throughout the next day, 27 February, things escalated rapidly. At noon, the Premier of NSW held a press conference saying they expected flood waters to be below the 2017 flood peak of 11.5 metres. Throughout the day, the Bureau of Meteorology continued to update its forecast for the peak flood height. Each time, the forecast was increasing. By 11 p.m., they predicted the river would breach the flood levee by 5 a.m. Evacuation orders were made for different areas during the day. At 4:10 p.m., an evacuation warning was issued for Lismore. At 9:30 p.m., an evacuation order was made for North and South Lismore. By 10:30 p.m., this evacuation order included the Lismore CBD. By the end of the day, Lismore had received 117.5mm of rain, and flood waters were at 12.3 metres.

On 28 February, Lismore recorded 557 mm of rain and flood waters were at 13.2 metres. At 2:30 a.m., the flood levee was breached. This resulted in the Lismore CBD being flooded. By 2 p.m. that day, the flood had peaked at 14 metres. River levels had risen so quickly that hundreds of people were trapped in their houses. The official rescue authority, the State Emergency Service (SES), was overwhelmed by the magnitude of the flood. Their resources were stretched and their volunteers could not operate effectively. Throughout the early morning, the community were responding to the disaster themselves. Aluminium, fishing boats (tinnies) and jet skis were used by community members to rescue stranded people, often ignoring directives from the SES not to do so. This is a common response to disasters. Usually, neighbours and other community members are on the scene and ready to help in an emergency. Part of this is due to local residents knowing the area, having the connections to pull a response together quickly, and already being there. Often, official formal responses may lack local knowledge and be led by people at a distance from the community.

After 11:50 p.m., the waters start to recede. But the water had to go somewhere, and towns downstream were flooded with people, once again being stranded. By 2 March, over 10,000 people had been made homeless in the Northern Rivers region of NSW by the floods.

While this flood was devastating, the rain returned 3 weeks later. This time, the town was traumatised. The situation was exacerbated by damaged and faulty emergency sirens, inaccurate flood gauges, poor weather forecasts and the SES putting an evacuation order in place, removing it, and then having to restate it some hours later.[128]

The community is stretched, suffering trauma and confused by the failure of the emergency services. Throughout both of these floods, the community were the first responders, helping each other out, even when they themselves were traumatised.

Rebuilding Traumatised Communities

Traumatised communities are not only those impacted by natural disasters like fire and floods. Communities can be traumatised for many reasons. They can become traumatised in the same way that individuals can be traumatised. People and communities can become traumatised by experiencing stress and life-threatening events without the essential buffering and support. This could be through war, poverty, crime or disaster.

The examples of Canberra and Lismore show communities impacted by events outside of their control that were life-threatening. For many, this stress will continue for weeks, months and years following the event. Rebuilding of the community is a priority after a disaster or another traumatic series of events. However, trauma poses some distinct challenges in both building and rebuilding communities. While community members are often the first responders in an emergency, they may be impacted by the event and suffering trauma themselves.

With the Lismore floods, 10,000 people were made homeless but many more were also impacted by the events. Professor James Bennett Levy (University of Sydney Centre for Rural Health) estimates that between 15–20,000 people were impacted by the floods with the community experiencing a collective trauma as well as people experiencing individual trauma. Research by Southern Cross University showed that nine months after the flood, 52% of those who lost housing were still living in the remains of their homes, over 25% were still in temporary accommodation (caravans, sheds, with friends and family, etc.), 18% were in insecure accommodation (tents, temporary rentals) and 4% had left the region. Many of these people were still waiting for government buybacks of properties and renovations a year after the floods. The same Southern Cross University survey showed that 20% were coping and 60% were not coping.[129] This ongoing stress only increases the depth and intensity of the trauma experienced by community members.

During and immediately following the event, people will pitch in and work together to help others and ensure the community survives. For the next few months, the focus will move on to what can be recovered from their homes and properties, finding temporary accommodation, and ensuring that they have enough food and care for themselves and their families. After six months, PTSD symptoms tend to set in, and people start experiencing anxiety-related symptoms and behaviours. When it impacts so many, as did the Lismore floods, the community may suffer collective trauma.

The usual approach in disaster recovery is a top-down approach. A range of professional agencies and services begin working with community members. A coordinator for the recovery may be appointed, counselling is made available, medical support is provided, a coordinated cleanup is initiated (this may include the use of the military to work alongside residents), government agencies commence assessing the recovery, initial funds are provided to support early recovery efforts, insurance claims are made, and government begins plans for recovery and rebuilding. This is all fine and good. It is necessary but it tends to leave the community out of the recovery process. An alternative approach is to harness the power of the community to aid in its own recovery. While this approach may be more time-consuming and require more flexibility, it will better prepare communities for future disasters and build greater community resilience.

An Asset-Based Community Development Approach to Healing Traumatised Communities

In 2014, a number of fires spread through the Gippsland region of Victoria. The East Gippsland Shire Council implemented the Adaption for Recovery project in Glenaladale, Bonang, Tubbut and Goongerah communities. This project was based on a modified asset-based community development (ABCD) approach. The usual response for disaster recovery is a deficits-and-needs-based approach, often relying on the expertise of agencies and services from outside the area. ABCD takes a much different approach. It is not interested in the deficits and perceived needs of a community but rather in identifying the assets available and then connecting and mobilising these to create change.

The Adaption for Recovery project appointed facilitators to lead the project in each community. The usual ABCD approach is to map the assets of the community; however, due to the disruption to normal community life caused by the fires, traditional mapping was not utilised. A modified approach to identifying the assets of each community was implemented, with each community identifying assets as their situation dictated.

No lives were lost to these fires, but many residences, buildings and other farming infrastructure had been damaged or destroyed, with a significant number of livestock killed. In one community, the fires had burned for 70 days, and 67 days in another. The loss of property, infrastructure and stock, and length of time the fires were burning had placed significant pressure on each community, with community members impacted psychologically and emotionally.

The Adaption for Recovery project had broad aims "to build resilience to natural hazards, by addressing adaptive capacity at the individual, family and community levels. It intended to move the community through recovery to resilience—as defined by each community."[130]

Facilitators were appointed for each community, and due to the project being community-directed (citizen-led), each project developed its own course. The council had allocated funding for the project to run over two years. Conditions for the funding were flexible to enable individual communities to determine where funds were to be allocated. Throughout 2016, the project was evaluated by the RMIT. Their evaluation report found:

- A number of diverse project activities occurred that increased both the individual capacity of community members and community preparedness for future disasters.
- A positive community response to project activities.
- Increased resilience in each community.
- Some residents reported an increased willingness to participate in community activities.
- An increased willingness to engage with government agencies and a greater level of trust in government.
- The ABCD approach had contributed to the positive results.[131]

Throughout the implementation of the project, many challenges arose. Where these could be dealt with by the mechanism of the project and the implementation of an ABCD approach, they were. The evaluation report found that ABCD provided a positive way to approach disaster recovery and build resilience. However, many approaches still rely on deficits-and-needs-based methodology. The Adaption for Recovery project model using a modified ABCD approach is an example of what can be achieved using a community-led and strengths-based approach to recovery.

Trauma-Informed Community Building

While not necessarily focused on communities experiencing trauma due to natural disasters, the Bridge Housing Corporation's trauma-informed community-building model is worth looking at.

The Bridge Housing Corporation is a not-for-profit organisation working to develop and provide affordable housing in the United States. In addition to the provision of housing, they also have a focus on building local communities. They are headquartered in San Francisco.

Bridge Housing Corporation developed the trauma-informed community-building model in partnership with the Health Equity Institute at San Francisco State University.

The model recognises that people experiencing trauma may have a reduced capacity to participate in building connected communities due to the impact of the traumatic events on their lives and their associated level of functioning. They may be experiencing long-term mental health conditions and their general sense of wellbeing may have deteriorated. Trauma could have disrupted their social networks and made it difficult for individuals and communities to identify issues that could be addressed to move forward. The capacity for the community to engage with further change processes and move forward may be severely reduced. The model's strategies aim to reduce the stress associated with traumatic events, create community cohesion and build resiliency so that community members are ready to work further on building their community.

The Bridge model identifies several barriers to building community capacity. These include:[132]

- **A diminished level of trust and lack of social cohesion**. Traumatic events can erode trust between people and highlight existing social divisions. Coping mechanisms are diminished with people often responding to the stress of trauma by further retreating into isolation. This lack of trust may be exacerbated by a history of intergenerational trauma, racism and other forms of discrimination.

- **Lack of stability, reliability and consistency**. Community members have often experienced unfulfilled promises for support and no longer trust agencies and others, leading to a reduced capacity to participate in community-building initiatives. They focus on their daily survival, ensuring their basic human needs are met first. Trauma will often leave them feeling further destabilised. The demands of undertaking a new role in rebuilding their community may be intimidating and further overwhelm them. They may withdraw from such activities.

- **People feeling disempowered and lacking community ownership**. Before the natural disaster, people may have experienced intergenerational trauma, racism, discrimination, inequality and other barriers to participation, such as poverty. Their social capital will already have been eroded, and they may have experienced failure by government and other agencies to invest in their community, a failure by authorities to listen to the community voice in the past, and they may be reluctant to further participate in actions to move forward.

- **Reduced capacity to imagine or envision the future.** People are overwhelmed by their trauma (past and present) and find it difficult to see past the current moment. This will limit their ability to imagine anything other than the current situation.
- **A high level of personal needs.** Community members are focused on their immediate survival needs of housing, food and financial security.
- **Depth and breadth of community needs.** Community building can only successfully occur when actions address their trauma. Some work has to be done in commencing to heal trauma before people will be in a position to move forward. Trauma can often leave a person feeling shame, guilt and low self-esteem. Long-term disadvantage and lack of investment in the community by the government adds to the trauma experienced when local agencies are unable to meet demands.

A trauma-informed approach does not aim to treat trauma directly. However, it welcomes people as they are, recognises the impact trauma has had on their lives and their capacity to participate, and it acknowledges the specific challenges a person faces. This forms a strong basis for action.

The Bridge model has four principles underlying its operation. These are the values guiding any work undertaken:

1. **Do no harm.** Any action undertaken must consider past and present trauma and its impact on individuals and the community. To achieve this, any activity must consider possible mental health triggers and be conducted in an environment where stress is reduced so that participants can be safe to fully engage and participate.

2. **Acceptance**. Participants are accepted for being where they are, recognising that trauma may manifest in various behaviours.

3. **Community empowerment.** The aim is for the community to be in a position to be in control and have a say in matters relating to them. Actions need to be inclusive and provide opportunities for community members to be supported in their participation.

4. **Reflective processes.** There is a recognition that trauma will take an extended period of time to heal. The Bridge approach allows for reflection on processes and actions to make the program flexible.

The Bridge model does not prescribe a set of strategies but has several intentional strategies to address trauma and its consequences so that community connection can commence. These intentional strategies are at the individual, interpersonal, community and systems levels. Many of these strategies could form the basis of any community-building initiative:[133]

Individual

This first level of intentional strategies is about building relationships with the individual and providing them with a basis to move forward in healing and working with others to build their community. It can be done by:

- **Providing opportunities for multiple interactions**. Working to create community change requires the building of honest relationships. This takes time and should happen in different environments.
- **Ensuring incentives and a sense of personal reward.** Incentives give the person a sense of achievement and help to retain their interest in the project.

- **Meeting residents where they are.** Trauma will manifest itself through some potentially dangerous, unhealthy and challenging behaviours. However, this does not mean the person lacks the gifts and skills to create a strong community.
- **Developing authentic relationships, setting realistic expectations and never overpromising.** No community-building action should promise something that is not achievable. To do this risks disappointment and the person becoming re-traumatised, and most importantly, it can cause real damage to the important relationship established.

Interpersonal

The interpersonal level of intentional strategies builds on the individual work and aims to build relationships between individuals so they are better prepared to build local communities. This interpersonal level comprises the following:

- **Modelling healthy behaviours.** The activities in a trauma-informed approach should be designed to allow positive healthy behaviours to be modelled so that they can be continued outside the program in the community and at home.
- **Supporting peer-to-peer activities and interactions.** These types of interactions help trauma-impacted people to regain some of their personal power. Working together with other community members on some activity, no matter how big or small, will assist in people being able to once again see the power they have when they work together with one another.
- **Providing opportunities that cultivate shared positive experiences.** Having positive experiences with others

builds social cohesion, the connection that has often become lost due to trauma. This is about rebuilding relationships and providing a safe place for people to heal.

- **Ensuring all activities allow for personal sharing and mutual support**. Personal sharing, even of what the person has taken from a joint activity, helps build bonds with others. It may even allow people to safely revisit their trauma and continue the healing process with the support of those around them.

Community

This level of strategy is aimed at building confidence with participants to begin creating a community and working together to face the challenges that come with trauma. It may require time and patience as often people have experienced programs or government initiatives that either failed to deliver on promises or finished before any realistic outcome was achieved. Community-based activities would involve:

- **Expanding efforts through incremental growth and building from success.** Change is a gradual process, particularly with a trauma-informed focus. Moving too quickly will place people at risk of becoming re-traumatised.
- **Ensuring that sustainability and quality are criteria for the implementation of community efforts.** Such activities will focus on the community taking ownership of all actions.
- **Providing visible, tangible activities that reflect community change.** This is achieved by involving community members in all decisions and actions developed. It provides an opportunity to reflect and celebrate what they have achieved together.

- **Cultivating community leadership through support and skill building.** All activities in the Bridge model are based on incremental changes and require support and skill-building at the individual and corporate levels to build leadership and confidence.

Systems

Making changes at the systems level provides a clear path for the community to take control of their destiny and gives them the power to move forward. This involves:

- **Reflecting community voices and priorities to stakeholders.** The Bridge model works with community members so that they can be their own advocates. It aims to empower them to speak up to authority to communicate their priorities for change and growth. This represents a system change. Not one created by government agencies, funding bodies and service providers, but by the community.
- **Building partnerships for long-term investments in community change and effective service delivery.** This is a real strength of the Bridge model. It aims to work with those agencies providing services and support to trauma-impacted communities so that they begin to partner with the community and work with them on the issues that matter most to them.
- **Advancing long-term community vision and developing a community-wide strategy to reach goals.** The Bridge model aims to encourage feedback from the community throughout each stage of the program. Alongside clear communication between the program and community, this helps to keep it on track to achieve its desired outcomes. It

185

empowers the community to be in a position where they can begin envisioning the future for their community and developing strategies to reach that vision.

We've seen two excellent approaches to working with trauma-impacted communities to help them heal from their trauma and move forward. The modified ABCD approach of both the Adaption for Recovery project and the Bridge model display empathy and are trauma-informed. Both display a willingness to listen to and hear from the community and work with them on a healing journey to rebuild strong, cohesive communities that will be in a position to face trauma more positively if and when it comes their way in the future. Both approaches build resilience and provide people with a way forward. They work to create community healing and the opportunity for individual healing within the community setting. Both approaches are also implemented after the events that created trauma. But what is happening to build resilience before communities are impacted by trauma?

Although many natural disasters provide little opportunity for preparation in the short-term (like earthquakes, freak storms and tsunamis that come with minimal warning and don't allow people time to prepare), there is a prior warning with other disasters. For example, we know that there is a time each year when there is potential for bush and forest fires. We have the opportunity to prepare for these events. Often, people will have a fire plan or an evacuation plan in place. I live in a tropical location with a cyclone risk each year. There is ample time in the dry season to prepare resources for a cyclone kit if a cyclone were to appear.

However, there is more we can do to be prepared for the impact of natural disasters and lower the risk of being impacted by trauma. So often, we are physically prepared, but is our community emotionally, psychologically and socially prepared for the event? Has the work been done to build a connected, strong community with resilience to better face the trauma that comes with the event? This is a known risk. How are we mitigating it?

Connected Communities and Natural Disasters

For some years, we have made our home in Far North Queensland in the Wet Tropics. Where we live is like many other villages, towns and cities in Australia and perhaps most of the Western world. Each day, people leave their homes for work, commuting in cars. Work is often in another suburb, the CBD or nearby towns. Once they arrive home, the garage door comes down and they settle in for an evening at home. Children often play indoors and people are rarely found in their front yards except to care for the garden or mow the lawns. We are blessed with a number of parks and walking tracks nearby. This allows for some exercise and some low-level engagement with others. Our climate of two seasons, the wet and the dry, encourages an outdoor lifestyle, but our connection with others is often limited largely due to our contemporary lifestyle. Like so many other villages, towns and cities, creating a strong connection with neighbours takes some work and, for many, appears to be difficult.

And like so many local government authorities, our council has moved away from grassroots community building and largely restricted its work to its core business that is often referred to as the 3 Rs: roads, rates and rubbish. In other words, providing basic services for the community to continue its existence. Many councils now no longer view community building as their role. As we'll see in a few moments, this is a mistake and, unfortunately, is quite common with many local government authorities. Many councils have adopted a corporate business model based on a neo-liberal philosophy. This approach sees councils operate more as a business and less as an organisation providing community services. This has resulted in a governance model that values physical outcomes over social outcomes. This common approach has missed some powerful opportunities to create better places for the whole community. It fails to appreciate that the mobilisation of a connected community has the potential to cut council costs due to the community being active in maintaining its own local physical space and having the potential to work on community building to create safer and friendlier places.

One thing my local council has done quite well is to maintain an active Disaster Management Unit. This is essential due to the Far North's history of damage and destruction caused by tropical cyclones, major flooding events and the occasional fire. With the reality of climate change, the chance of a cyclone impacting the city in the wet season has increased. Meteorologists tell us that if and when one does develop in the Coral Sea, it will be more intense with greater unpredictability than previous cyclonic events. Of course, this risk is reflected in high home and property insurance premiums.

The Disaster Management Unit operates throughout the year, not only when there is a disaster or at the time of the year when the risk is higher. For example, during the dry season, preparation is made for the next wet season with training programs and resilience-building initiatives. One or two positions in the unit are dedicated to resilience building throughout the year. This is important due to the potential community and social disruption that a cyclone could cause. Often, the recovery takes years rather than months following such an event.

Resilience-building work involves the Disaster Management Unit working closely with community services organisations and agencies in building their capacity to respond to a disaster, conducting community-building activities and working to ensure a process where the most vulnerable community members are cared for in the event of a disaster. Building communities between disasters is critical work. It provides the community's residents with a greater sense of resilience, positioning the community to deal with major trauma from a stronger place. Additionally, creating connected communities can mean local response is enhanced and resilience to rebuild is developed.

As I write this, events have been unfolding on the island of Maui in Hawaii where a major fire has destroyed a heritage-listed area frequented by tourists. As the fatality numbers continue to rise, the community is devastated, asking how it could have happened and why disaster-warning systems seem to have failed. Rebuilding this town and community will take some time. Hopefully, there are already connected networks of residents, so they won't have to rebuild and reform social connections. Community members are understandably traumatised. The coming days, weeks, months and years may be quite difficult. Many will have lost friends and neighbours. They will be grieving not only the loss of their home and town but also the loss of valuable community members. Some will choose to move on and start again in another location. For those who remain, the task of rebuilding will be daunting. They will be dealing with grief, guilt and trauma when physically rebuilding their community. They will struggle with government resources overwhelmed by the tragedy, insurance agencies, and other unforeseen struggles. Rebuilding will take time and hard work. Having a connected community before the disaster would provide a basis to move forward; building one afterwards is now an essential task.

The Foundation for Rural & Regional Renewal

The Foundation for Rural & Regional Renewal in Bendigo has observed that those communities with a high level of social connections, where there is an observable presence of strong social capital, who are inclusive with a diversity of leadership as well as being engaged in the disaster management systems, are in a better position than other communities when it comes to disaster recovery.[134]

However, many approaches to preparation for disaster are top-down approaches. As much as the approach of councils providing resilience officers to build capacity is a positive move, it often is represented in a top-down form. The focus will be on building the capacity of local services at the cost of building a sense of local community and resilience through the community taking the lead or being equal partners in disaster preparation.

When a community-led approach to preparation is undertaken, the community works as partners with the official disaster-management resources. In this sense, the communities work with the disaster- management officers in building their local capacity to respond successfully to a disaster.[135] If this is the case, the community can fully participate in decisions that impact them.

However, disaster-management committees often make these decisions, not the potentially impacted community.

Between 2017 and 2020, the Foundation for Rural & Regional Renewal and Resilience NSW worked on a pilot-research program with three different NSW communities at high risk of various disaster scenarios. They examined the impact of community-led preparation for these disasters. Potential disasters included flood, fire, storm, drought and heat waves.

Researchers used an action-research model based on the question: how and to what extent do community-led approaches enable local communities to be better prepared for disasters? In the project, researchers worked alongside communities to support a co-design approach in developing their local response to disaster. Each community worked autonomously to create their specific approaches.

One community focused on working to connect neighbours to build a strong community and develop children's skills as leaders. Another focused on celebrating the area's local culture through the development of arts-based communities and culture trails. A third approach was on local mapping and developing youth as leaders. While this was occurring, researchers maintained their concentration on key resilience markers. These markers included communication, networks, self-organising systems, decision making, information, resources, tools, support and inclusion.[136]

Research from the project has produced some interesting findings. These findings should help support greater work in building connected communities in between disasters so that government and other disaster-response services are not left struggling to provide an adequate response to these events.

Their findings were as follows:[137]

1. **Resilience is not something individuals or communities can achieve independently.** It is developed through the interplay of systems, processes, networks (formal and informal) and community support working together. It happens as a result of a collective effort. This involves government, agencies, community organisations and individuals collaborating. Researchers noted that the community and community organisations are often left out of planning and response preparation. This leaves a gap in the building of individual and community resilience.

2. **Communities were very willing and able to participate as equal collaborators in resilience-building efforts.** There is a real opportunity for planning for disasters and resilience building where community groups and individuals could participate. Often, they are waiting to be asked to be involved.

3. **Emergency management agencies have an opportunity to engage with communities to build trust and collaboration, which is essential in resilience-building efforts.** This finding indicates a change from a top-down process to one where communities become active partners.

4. **Local government is ideally placed to support ongoing resilience-building work alongside local communities.** Local government is already an active player in disaster management and preparation. This finding allows local governments to focus on their role as community builders. This may require a change in policy for many local councils and may be quite challenging for more traditionally minded councils who see their role mainly in terms of providing physical infrastructure and essential services such as waste management. In Australia, the situation varies from state to state and council to council. Some states require councils to report on their work with communities, while others have no such legislative requirement.

   For example, at one time, Queensland councils were required to prepare a community development plan and then report to the state government on their actions to meet the goals and strategies in that plan. This is no longer a requirement. The result is that some councils still maintain a plan and actively participate in community development actions. In contrast, others have abandoned it and no longer provide community development services, focusing more on building community through providing and maintaining physical infrastructure. The challenge of this finding is for councils to conduct some real grassroots work in building connected communities, with one aspect of this work being resilience building. This will require a further change of the organisational mindset from seeing communities as passive recipients of services to one where communities lead and are active, independent participants in planning and programs.

5. **Community sector organisations already have a strong track record in activating and mobilising through their local relationships in disaster response and recovery** (particularly local and locally based organisations, including neighbourhood and community centres). Community organisations often already have established networks and links with their local communities. This asset is often overlooked in current disaster-planning actions and resilience building. These organisations are often already first responders in the event of a disaster and could be active participants in any disaster-planning and management processes.

6. **State governments have a central strategic role to play in supporting community-led disaster-resilience initiatives.** They can do this via working with emergency-management agencies and other government departments involved in emergency management. This highlights the importance of state governments' strategic role in disaster management preparation. The role of community-led responses will require this to be included in state governments' strategic planning and resourcing.

From these findings, the researchers also made some important recommendations to facilitate a different approach to disasters and the resilience building of communities:[138]

1. **Community-led approaches.** These need to become central to disaster preparation and resilience building.

2. **New structures and processes.** A different way ahead in disaster planning must be developed, recognising the community and individual community members as equal contributors in disaster preparation and response.

3. **Shared responsibility.** A new emphasis on shared responsibility between existing disaster- planning agencies and communities must result in support for community-led planning and actions to develop local resilience.

4. **Resilience building needs to include community knowledge and experience.** Regardless of formal processes, communities and community members will continue working on their resilience-building and rebuilding actions. This needs to be recognised and supported in formal responses.

5. **Engagement between disaster events.** The period between one disaster and the next provides a real opportunity for true engagement between communities and planning authorities. This will assist in the development of resilience and cooperation when the next disaster occurs.

6. **Communities and information provision.** Community agencies and organisations can play an active role in structuring information distribution to reflect local considerations.

7. **Resourcing and investment.** There is a recognition that community-led efforts are important and require resourcing and investment. Without ongoing investment,

disaster- planning responses can only be weakened with past mistakes being repeated.

8. **Community-led resilience occurs in a complex system.** Researchers recognised that for community-resilience development to be successful, it requires support from a complex network of relationships and networks. It requires a systems-planning approach. Resilience building needs to consider that issues such as isolation, economic disadvantages and conflict within the community all contribute to a high risk in a disaster response. It should be recognised that issues like this, while unrelated to the disaster itself, all increase the impact of the disaster and that resilience planning needs to recognise these issues and account for their impact in planning.

9. **Supporting negotiated partnerships.** Researchers recommended a focus on supporting links that already exist between local systems, community organisations, networks and other locally based groups in building local resilience.

This is an important piece of research in disaster planning, response and resilience. It recognises the importance of connected communities and existing networks in building resilience and that it can be enhanced by including these networks and communities in existing planning frameworks. There is a recognition that the current planning systems are missing the important component of community- led resilience actions. It adds to the understanding that when a disaster impacts a community, all are in it together and need each other's support. Working with the existing community networks and building stronger communities through community-led responses will lead to a stronger and more connected community better prepared to deal with the trauma associated with disaster and loss. This will lead to healing for impacted individuals and communities.

A New Way Forward?

In a natural disaster, we are all in it together. We don't need to look very far to see how traumatic a natural disaster can be, and that recovery can take several years. Impacted communities can be devastated, with trauma being prominent.

We've outlined several trauma-informed approaches to working with trauma-impacted communities in rebuilding them and working together to become more resilient both individually and as a community. It is long-term work with physical, social, community, emotional and psychological facets all requiring attention. Often, the emphasis is on the immediate physical concerns and initial support to cope economically and psychologically.

There are three emerging actions from the research of approaches and the stated experience of community members.

The first is in healing individuals and their communities following a disaster. Several approaches have been used. What is common to them is that they will always need to be trauma-informed and working with people to do no harm. There is a clear recognition that the existing community networks, assets, strengths and local organisations are all essential inclusions in a process of recovery, healing and resilience building. This requires a partnership approach where the community's wishes are paramount and can only move forward at the speed the community is happy with. It cannot be rushed, as every individual and every community will be different. Those with strong connection and high social capital prior to a disaster will be in a much stronger position to move forward than those with poor social cohesion. Healing will progress through the professional supports offered and, importantly, from the growing community as people heal together. The work of rebuilding a community and healing from a major traumatic event is one of those times when the community will want support from others. Often, people may not take up the offer of professional support and will work to heal their trauma through their interactions with others. Some of these interactions may be informal such as discussions with friends and colleagues where trauma can be revisited in short, sustainable bursts or more formally through prayer groups, support groups and other social mechanisms. Building resilience is something that we all do together and it relies on several factors. It is not something we do ourselves.

The second priority is building a sense of connected community between disaster events. As we have seen, these can be unpredictable and not necessarily something we can timetable. As we are all observing, they appear to be growing more intense in their impact. Several approaches have been outlined from the Bridge program, the experience in Gippsland and the research conducted in NSW. Common among these are the importance of building a connected and strong community between disasters and the need to work together to build community and individual resilience. Local knowledge and experience are essential while recognising a community's existing strengths and assets to provide a building block to a stronger community.

The third priority is for planning bodies and organisations to change their focus from a top-down approach and recognise the wealth of knowledge and experience coming from the community. This requires a more grassroots approach to disaster preparation and will necessarily include community representatives in the planning processes. It is important that those involved in these processes recognise the potential for a power imbalance in the local disaster committee. It can be quite intimidating for community representatives to be involved in a committee where quite powerful organisations outnumber them. This is another challenge for those involved in disaster processes to ensure that community voices are heard and attended to. Associated with the composition of local disaster-management committees is the gender imbalance. So many of the organisations involved are male-dominated at their management level, resulting in female representatives and their voices often missing from the planning response. We have not discussed this in reviewing the research, but it is an important component in developing an adequate response. A better gender balance in the committees and organisations involved in the preparation and response committees will ensure that issues previously overlooked due to this imbalance can be addressed. This is another challenge that must be addressed as we move forward in our responses to disasters.

Allied with community rebuilding is the priority for local governments to be involved in community development activities between disasters. This is often a missing ingredient in building social cohesion. But local government is best placed to complete this necessary task. They are the level of government closest to the community with local knowledge. They can provide a powerful resource in building communities and community-led responses to issues arising in the event of a disaster. The ongoing work of community building between disasters is an issue that should take a higher priority for local government, However, it is often overlooked due to the contemporary focus of local government on being creators of physical assets and money managers, while neglecting the importance of building the community.

Without making these changes, our response to disasters and preparing impacted communities for the following trauma will be limited. We will always find ourselves acting reactively rather than proactively to recover.

CHAPTER 14:

Welcoming the Stranger

"Do not forget to show hospitality to strangers, for by so doing some people have shown hospitality to angels without knowing it."
Hebrews 13:2

Many of us would be familiar with the parable of Jesus about the Good Samaritan. Jesus was responding to the question, "Who is my neighbour?" He told about a man travelling from Jerusalem to Jericho who was attacked, stripped and robbed. He was left by the side of the road to die. A priest passed by and walked on the other side of the road. Similarly, a Levite did the same thing. But a Samaritan stopped, cared for the man and left him in the care of others with the promise that on his return, he would compensate any costs of those caring for the man. The Samaritan had no reason to stop. Jews and Samaritans would usually avoid each other if they could. However, he took the time to care for the stranger and ensure his wellbeing. At the end of the story, Jesus asked the questioner who the man's neighbour was. Of course, the answer was the Samaritan who had shown compassion to someone he did not know. The story can be found in the New Testament Gospel of Luke in Chapter 10, verses 25–37.

The question for us is, would we do the same thing? Would we go out of our way for a stranger to show them care, to help them heal?

A recent post on the social media page of the group for the suburb where I live stated the following: *Guy scoping out houses around ....Indigenous, late 20's, dreads, orange sports singlet, black shorts, black baseball cap on a black bike. Came to the door asking for someone, "must have the wrong address."*

This post assumes that the person is checking out houses for a future break-in attempt and not that he was looking for someone and may have had the wrong address. Is this the way your neighbourhood would address a stranger in your street? Not the welcoming approach advocated by both Jesus and the writer of the New Testament book of Hebrews. The first comment in the discussion was, *Did you call the police?* Again, this reinforces the assumption the man was a potential criminal. This is a long way from seeing the stranger as a possible angel.

There is tension between welcoming the stranger and recognising a risk to the community. As much as we are hardwired to want to connect with others, we also are hardwired for a survival instinct, and when confronted with a potential threat, our fight or flight stress response will be activated. We can see others outside of our community as a risk. We also need to connect with others for our own safety. This is the basis for the "tribe" (the community), but at the same time, we feel a need to protect that tribe or community from those who might pose a risk to its survival. It is a judgement we all make on an ongoing basis, but when it becomes driven by fear, it can lock us away from others.

We must find the balance between self-protection and welcoming others into our community.

In this chapter, we will discuss concepts around a connected community, and being a community exhibiting hospitality to others, including the stranger. It is a community that welcomes the "other", the person who is different from us, while recognising the tension between safety and danger.

A connected, healing community is an inclusive community where all are welcome. This will mean divesting ourselves of existing prejudices and images of people. Once we have done this, we can begin to invite them into our community. We stop seeing the person as an "other", but as another who has gifts and skills instead, just as you and I have gifts and skills. An example of this in action is the changing societal view of people with disabilities. A generation ago, many people with disabilities were locked away in institutions. They were not often seen in the outside world and treated as inferior or disabled. But thanks to some strong advocacy by people with disabilities and their support groups, legislation is now in place to treat them with dignity and respect. Many of the institutions where so many were housed are now closed, and people with disabilities live in the community. Although our response is sometimes not perfect, we are now encouraged to see the person as another person with abilities and skills in the same way that we have abilities and skills. We are so much richer for having people with disabilities as part of our communities. Access for a person with a disability means better access for all of us, and the diversity of a society welcoming people who have a disability makes us all richer.

Diversity is one of the strengths of a connected community. Without diversity, our community ceases to be a place where healing can occur but becomes an inward-looking space where people are busy protecting what they already have and living their communal lives with fear-based responses. As we have outlined in earlier chapters, a connected community is a safe community. Connection with neighbours and keeping our street active creates a safe street. Our safety comes from this connection from the relationships we establish with each other. This connection is enhanced by joining in activities such as street get-togethers and actions like park cleanups. It is the things we do together that create deeper relationships with our neighbours and help to make our community a safe place.

Further, the recognition that all of us have gifts, skills and experiences to enhance our community is an opportunity to deepen our community and create an even safer place. Once we start seeing the assets and strengths in our neighbours, we can see the assets and potential in those who are more marginalised in our neighbourhoods. We can stop seeing youth as a problem but as potential. They represent our future and often have the ability to envision a better future than some of us older community members can. Instead of seeing youth on our streets as a problem, they can become participants in creating a safe place. Youth have very few options for meeting together other than to use public space. It is a free space and they can use it to bond with each other. Just as spending more time in the front yard creates greater surveillance, having youth in our streets just "hanging out" creates another form of surveillance. They are one of our greatest resources in creating a safe place.

Once we have a connected community, perhaps instead of immediately calling the police when we encounter a stranger, a better approach may be to enter into a discussion with the stranger. Of course, if you feel at risk or unsafe, then call the police. Returning to the example of a man knocking on the door of a house in my suburb and being turned away, a better approach may have been to talk to the stranger about who they were looking for, where they might live and how you could help them find the person. As well as being more inclusive and inviting the person into a discussion, this would have provided the opportunity to assess if the person was scoping the neighbourhood for a future break-in or was simply looking for a friend.

Just as our neighbours are strangers until we meet them and invite them into our lives through a discussion and building a relationship, the same exists for any stranger. They will always be a potential risk until we invite them into our lives through simple conversation. At the heart of a strong community is connection and belonging. We start to belong when we connect with others. The stranger stops being a threat or a risk when we invite them in by initiating a simple conversation.[139]

Hospitality

Hospitality is a gift and a hallmark of a strong, connected and inclusive community. Welcoming our neighbours into our lives is the start of building this community. Each small interaction builds the relationship that helps us build our local community, our village. The community is strengthened by what we do together and for each other. This can be as simple as helping a neighbour with a repair, organising a street get-together, collecting the mail when a neighbour is away, and welcoming new residents into our community. This is where hospitality starts (i.e., how we bring others, our neighbours, into our world). This is the beginning of the community where we live. I recall when we moved to our first rented house after we had relocated to Far North Queensland. Our first visitor was our neighbour, who called in to welcome us as we were unpacking after moving into the house. He left a card with his name and telephone number on it. This simple action of hospitality and neighbourliness made us feel at home, part of the street and the community.

In our modern, fast-paced, consumerist world, we barely have time to socialise with our friends, let alone invite strangers into our homes. As highlighted earlier in this book, we are not as socially connected as we once were, and we don't show the same level of hospitality to even our closest friends as we did just a few decades ago. Our lives are cluttered and busy. At the same time, we have devalued hospitality to being paid service for food, drink and other services. We don't value it the same way that our forebears, or even our parents, valued it. At the start of this chapter, we quoted from the Christian New Testament to introduce hospitality. It was a concept at the heart of early Christianity. It is also part of many other faith traditions, communities and cultures. In the past, hospitality was viewed as an essential element of society. At its heart is treating the stranger in the same way you would treat friends and family. The person acting as the host would provide for the physical and emotional needs of the guest. This would include food, shelter and friendship without expecting anything in return. It was understood that the stranger may host in return at a future time.[140]

The wonderful thing about hospitality is that it can be expressed in many forms. While it may mean welcoming a stranger or a guest into our homes, it can often be much simpler. It is about reaching out to those on our margins. Sometimes, they may be our neighbours and new acquaintances, but they can also be those with whom we would not normally socialise or even consider socialising. It is a state of mind of us accepting others without judging them. Acceptance can be done in small ways. It could mean simply listening to their story or offering them a lift or a drink. It is welcoming the stranger into our world. It takes us out of our comfort zones, extends us, and as we know, every conversation and experience changes us and provides an opportunity for our brains to rewire, even in the smallest way. Lisa Kentgen says it so well: "In its highest form, hospitality breaks down the wall that separate us, nurturing the spirit of community and a sense of belonging in both host and guest"[141] We can start this process with our neighbours. Some are easier than others to welcome into our world.

The easy ones are the ones we readily enjoy chatting to and getting to know. We would be quite open to sitting down for a meal or a coffee with them and sharing our stories. But the challenge comes when we extend that circle a bit further to those neighbours we don't readily identify with. Extending ourselves to meet with these neighbours in a deeper discussion and inviting them into our community will take us a little more out of our comfort zone. We could extend this a little further and show how hospitable we can be to others. For example, to people experiencing homelessness, to the young person who feels so traumatised by his home experience that he spends time out in the street with his friends, or to the stranger who comes to our door looking for a friend only to realise they are at the wrong address.

Being hospitable takes effort and it takes time. Many conversations with friends, neighbours and strangers are unplanned. They happen in the moment. But often we are so busy that we miss the opportunity to share in another person's life. Building connections and community is a commitment of time and being present in the moment.

Hospitality is also something that doesn't come naturally to most of us. It is a skill to learn and develop. As it happens in the moment, we need to start from where we are. One conversation, one invitation at a time. With each hospitable moment, we open ourselves up to more opportunities. In our modern lives, this is not easy. We live busy lives. We come home, lock ourselves away in our houses and are glued to our technology. But once we take the first step, we are on the road to being more hospitable. The more we connect with others, the more we want to connect. It takes one small step at a time. While it takes us outside our comfort zone, we need to know and observe what our limits are to retain our sense of being safe. If we start feeling stressed and drained, we need to pull back. We should feel extended but not unsafe. Sometimes, finding this limit will be difficult and will depend on what is happening in our daily lives.

Volunteering: An Entry Point for Hospitality

If we are unfamiliar with hospitality, it might be worthwhile to find a simple entry point. One avenue to start growing a sense of hospitality is volunteering. This is a simple way to extend ourselves and become open to others. The great thing is that it doesn't even have to take up a great amount of time. It also provides us with a sense of giving back to our community and can teach us much in return. Scheduling even a couple of hours each week to volunteer for a community organisation helps us break down our locked front-door barrier and extend our networks. Moreover, our society values volunteering, so it won't make you feel out of place.

There are many reasons why a person may choose to volunteer. Let's consider some of these:

- Personal satisfaction. Just feeling good about offering your time to help others. Helping others is part of our hardwired drive to connect with others.
- Giving back to the community.
- Social contact. It's a great and simple way to combat isolation and loneliness.
- Remaining active.
- Making use of our skills. Many volunteers have a wealth of experience and skills. Volunteering can help to keep these skills fine-tuned.
- Learning new skills. Volunteering provides you with new experiences and an opportunity to learn something new.

- Gaining work experience. This is often a reason why young people volunteer: to gain experience for their resume. Others volunteer to get experience in a new career path. A former colleague of mine in local government commenced volunteering to improve disability access in his community and to aid his recovery from a major injury. After working as a volunteer in disability access, he had enough experience to gain a position as a disability and inclusion officer with the council.

A few years ago, I had the opportunity to volunteer for a local suicide-prevention organisation. I had just finished a lengthy period of employment in local government and wanted to use my skills. One thing I could offer was help with grant applications. In my previous local-government role, I had successfully applied for several grants. To offer this skill as a volunteer was an easy entry for me into the organisation and to be a volunteer. I spent one morning a week researching grant opportunities and completing applications. The organisation depended on grant funding to continue its work, so this volunteering contributed to its ongoing viability. In return, the organisation provided all its volunteers with free mental health first aid training. So, the experience was rewarding for both the organisation and me as a participant. They had grant applications lodged with funding bodies, and I had gained a qualification I had wanted for a few years.

There are many volunteering opportunities in the local community. They can be found in sporting bodies, charities, not-for-profit organisations, arts groups, thrift shops and local government, to name a few.

Many councils operate volunteer programs for their art galleries, community facilities, community groups and environmental programs. Many people volunteer for an organisation that shares their interests, experience and passions. Many find volunteering for a Men's Shed or community garden to be rewarding and find others with mutual interests.

Some years ago, I volunteered for a local community radio station. I had a passion for music, but finding performance opportunities was limited due to my workload. I became involved with a local community radio station, starting as an announcer for a folk-music program. This was a rewarding experience as I could simply share my passion for the musical genre by sitting behind a microphone and playing music to others. A bit like sitting around at home and sharing new music with friends. After some time, I volunteered for the management board of the station. For me, this was a valuable experience. I learnt valuable lessons in how community organisations functioned while providing a service to others. Like many other volunteering experiences, the community radio station formed a tight-knit community for its volunteers. People were there for so many reasons. Many were there, like me, for the love of music. Others were frustrated amateur radio announcers, and some were there to provide an alternative to the local commercial station, while others were there for the learning experience and to form the launching pad for a career in media. We all were quite different and possibly would never have crossed paths with each other if it hadn't been for the radio station. And like many communities, we fulfilled so many functions for each other, including the opportunity for healing together.

There are several other volunteering opportunities, and those that are a little quirkier and more unusual may be the perfect opportunity for some. For example, a local model-train group was looking for a place to meet, set up their trains for use and to interest others. The local shopping centre had a shop that had recently become vacant. They set the trains and tracks up in this shop with two working railway lines. The open shop has provided them with an opportunity to call in while they are shopping and to entertain children and other model rail enthusiasts with their working trains. I have no doubt that this has increased their membership and provided them with a friendly environment to conduct their hobby. It is a passion-driven opportunity for volunteers. And they certainly need passionate volunteers to ensure the doors stay open.

Activities such as this provide a simple opportunity to become involved in volunteering and they make for an easy entry to extending hospitality to strangers. They also enrich our community, providing opportunities for connection and healing for both the volunteer and those people the volunteer encounters. It can be a mutually beneficial experience.

Unfortunately, as with so many other aspects of our society, our busy lifestyle is reflected in a reduced number of us who find time to be volunteers. In the 2016 Census, 19% of Australians indicated they volunteered in some way or another. By the 2021 Census, this percentage had dropped to 14.1%. This may have been due to the impact of the COVID-19 pandemic or a decreased level of social cohesion and connection.[142]

Volunteering is one way to start the practice of hospitality. However, it is only one entry point. There are many others. Whichever path you choose to start extending hospitality, it grows your own capacity and skills and adds to a strong community. A community reflecting the values of hospitality is one open to diversity. It celebrates the differences and the things shared in common between the members of that community and those they welcome.

One underlying value of being a community exhibiting hospitality to others is creating a welcoming space for everyone. To quote from the not-for-profit organisation Welcome America: "Being welcoming is more than being tolerant—it's having a true respect and appreciation of our neighbours and making sure that, in our culture and in our policies, everyone belongs."[143]

The questions for each of us now are: Are we exhibiting the value and gift of hospitality? Or are we closing the door to the stranger in our midst? If so, is my community truly connected, welcoming and diverse?

The Refugee Question

Any discussion of welcoming the stranger would not be complete without consideration of welcoming the refugee and asylum-seeker. A Google search of "welcoming the stranger" brings up 14,600,000 entries. Many of these entries refer to welcoming the refugee or the asylum-seeker. The stranger in a strange land. Many are from faith-based agencies, but others are from government departments, refugee advocates and general community members.

As with welcoming the stranger into our personal world and local community, there is a tension between the stated values of a nation and the operation of immigration, refugee and asylum-seeker policies. Although many nations are secular states where religion is separated from the operation of government, there are close historical ties to religion and the nation's development. This is particularly true for nations with colonial links to European powers. While it could be anticipated that there would be an alignment with the faith-based sentiment to welcome the stranger, this is tempered by the nation's political, economic, social and military experience, as well as its current political policies.

As we've discussed earlier, Australia, like so many other colonised countries, has a poor record regarding its treatment of the land's Indigenous inhabitants. This approach has not been restricted to the Indigenous population but also often been reflected in official policy and government approaches to refugees and asylum-seekers. While some of this may be a reflection of the community values of the time, it has frequently been at odds with international agreements and covenants signed by representatives of the Australian government and ratified by parliament.

As a unified nation, Australia came into being on 1 January, 1901. Before this time, it was a collection of individual English colonies, each with its own government. Becoming a federation was a hard- fought political and social battle, with Western Australia being the last to agree to join the other colonies in forming a federated nation.

Let's briefly summarise the development of the Australian government's approaches to immigrants, refugees and asylum-seekers. This will set the scene for further discussion of the concept of welcoming the stranger.

Immigration Before 1901

Australia as an English colonial settlement was first established as a penal colony. But by the mid-1850s, Australia had become a popular destination for free settlers (i.e., those who were not transported as a penalty for criminal behaviour). The discovery of gold in 1851 accelerated interest in people immigrating to Australia. Although many had come from England, a significant number of settlers came from Ireland, Scotland, Wales, the USA, China and Germany. But not all were equally welcome. In particular, Chinese immigrants faced a much more difficult entry than European or American immigrants. Governments placed barriers to their entry. For example, the Victorian government placed a poll tax of £10 per head on Chinese passengers disembarking. Many attempted to avoid this tax by disembarking in another colony and walking to the Victorian goldfields instead.[144] Tension between Chinese immigrants and other colonists lasted for many years, with this tension at times boiling over to acts of violence.

Federation to World War II

In 1901, the newly formed Australian government passed the Immigration Restriction Act. The White Australia policy informed this legislation. This policy aimed to restrict entry to Australia to those of European background. In operation, this exclusion was made possible by a dictation test. Those wanting to enter Australia had to write and sign a passage of 50 words in a European language as instructed by an immigration officer. The test was first given in English. If the applicant passed but was considered racially or politically unacceptable, the test was administered again in another European language. Between 1902 and 1903, the test was given 805 times, with only 46 people passing. Between 1904 and 1909, it was administered another 554 times, with just 6 people passing. Those failing the test were excluded from Australia and deported. After 1909, no person passed the test.

The Immigration Restriction Act remained in force until 1958 when the dictation test was abolished. However, the White Australia policy remained part of Australian political and social life until 1975 when the Racial Discrimination Act officially made it a thing of the past.[145]

Following World War I, the Australian government had sought an increase in immigration, intending to grow the population to provide protection should a future war break out. On first hearing this reaction to the First World War, it may seem to be an odd decision. A common misunderstanding is that the war was fought only in Europe. Australia did lose a large number of young men to the war and many died in battles on European soil. However, the first Australian casualties in World War I were not those at Gallipoli in Turkey or France. The first Australian soldiers to be casualties lost their lives in Papua New Guinea. These lives were lost in the Battle of Bita Paka on September 11, 1914. This battle was fought to gain control of the German-controlled wireless station at Bita Paka near Rabaul. This was seven months before the well-known ANZAC campaign at Gallipoli in Turkey.

World War I signalled a change to the dominance of colonial powers in the Pacific Ocean. Before the war, Germany had colonial control of New Guinea, among other holdings. At the war's end, they lost control of these locations, with Australia taking control of Papua New Guinea. The war also saw the rise of Japan as a political influence in the Pacific region.

In this situation, it is understandable that the Australian government would want to boost the population to protect the mainland from invasion by a foreign force. The government also needed to boost the Australian labour force as so many young men had died in the war.

Unsurprisingly with the White Australia policy, they looked to Great Britain for this population boost and offered prospective immigrants assisted passage. As a further enticement, British immigrants were also offered land grants and encouraged to take labouring jobs in rural and regional areas. Starting in 1922, the British Empire Settlement Act assisted over 200,000 British immigrants to start a new life in Australia over the next ten years.[146]

Post-World War II

The Second World War disrupted migration to Australia.

Following the war, the Australian government again campaigned to bring migrants to Australia. Parts of mainland

Australia had been under attack during the war. The government wanted to boost the population once again to protect the nation from future invasions and to provide a labour force. They used the slogan "Populate or Perish" to promote their campaign.

The first wave of immigration was displaced people from Eastern Europe wanting a new start. Their homes had been destroyed by war and national borders had been redrawn, with the United Soviet Socialist Republic (USSR) exerting influence and control over much of Eastern Europe. Between 1947 and 1953, 170,000 displaced persons settled in Australia.

The second wave of mass migration to Australia was during the 1950s and 60s. During this time, only half of those migrating to Australia were British with the balance made up of people largely from Greece, Italy, Turkey, Malta and Croatia. Many of these migrants were seeking employment and improved lives.

Migration has generally continued at a lower level since the 1960s.[147]However, following the COVID-19 pandemic, migration numbers have spiked with 737,000 migrants arriving in 2022/23. The previous year 427,000 arrived in Australia. This represents a 71% increase. It should be noted that 554,000 of these migrants were only on temporary visas. This included 283,000 who were international students, 70,000 working holiday makers and 49,000 temporary skilled workers. [148]

Contemporary Situation

In 1973, the Migration Act was amended to reflect a non-discriminatory immigration policy, and in 1975, the Racial Discrimination Act saw the end of the White Australia policy. In 2022/23 there were 195,004 permanent migrants to Australia.[149] These are accepted under four main categories:

- Skilled migration. This is targeted migration to attract migrants with skills required for the Australian economy.

- Family reunion. A scheme to bring family members of those already immigrated to Australia.
- Humanitarian migration. This is aimed to resettled those who are refugees and seeking asylum in Australia.

Special eligibility migration. This targets special skills, often in the artistic and sporting fields.[150]

Refugees and Asylum-Seekers

There are now more dislocated people fleeing their homeland due to persecution, violence, human- rights abuse, economic challenges and natural disasters than there were following World War II. There are almost 26 million refugees, almost half of whom are aged under 18. In recent years, those seeking resettlement in Australia have come from the following countries and regions: the Middle East, Afghanistan, Central Africa, Sudan, Eritrea, Somalia, Myanmar and Bhutan.[151]

Australia is a signatory to the 1951 United Nations Convention Relating to the Status of Refugees. It is also a signatory to the 1967 Protocol Relating to the Status of Refugees. The protocol defines a refugee as "a person who has a well-founded fear of persecution for reasons of race, religion, nationality, membership of a particular social group or political opinion."[152] Under this protocol, once a person has been classified as a refugee by the United Nations, they must not be returned to a place where they could face further persecution based on any grounds found in the protocol. This is referred to as "refoulement".

There is some confusion for many around the terms "asylum-seeker" and "refugee". An asylum-seeker is a person seeking refuge whose request has not yet been assessed. Asylum-seekers are requesting protection from conflict, persecution or violence due to their race, religion or political opinion. The person seeking asylum must wait until their request for protection has been assessed and the country where they have sought protection grants them the status of refugee. All refugees are asylum-seekers, but not all are classified as refugees until their claim has been processed and accepted. Every year, over 1 million people request asylum. Due to the slow speed of processing, in 2018, there were 3.5 million people internationally waiting for this processing to occur.[153] For some it can be a very long wait.

In straightforward terms:

- A refugee is someone who has left their country of origin, is living elsewhere and has been granted asylum by another country.
- An asylum-seeker is a person waiting for their claim to be assessed.[154]

Let's clarify a few confusing points around the issue of refugees and asylum-seekers, as so many poor assumptions have been made regarding this:

1. It is not illegal to seek asylum in another country.
2. It is not illegal to arrive in another country without a passport or visa and claim asylum.
3. An asylum-seeker is not an immigrant, as migrants leave a country through their own free choice.[155]

Australia has operated a highly controversial offshore processing scheme. While it is not illegal to seek asylum in Australia without a valid visa, those who do so are subject to mandatory detention. Australia has operated a system of mandatory detention since 1992, and under the Migration Act of 1958, anyone without a valid visa must be detained. Those in detention can only be released if granted a valid visa or expelled from the country.

At the end of January 2023, there were 1,061 people in immigration-detention facilities in Australia. Another 516 had been approved to live in the community; 146 were children. A further 10,728 were classified as "Unauthorised Maritime Arrivals" (i.e., they had arrived by boat and lived in the community under bridging visas). 1,334 of these were children.[156] The average period of time a person spends in detention is 806 days (2.2 years), with over half being in detention for over a year.

This is one of the harshest immigration systems operating in the world, and unfortunately, it is being seen by some countries as a model to follow. As well as representing mandatory detention, there is no time limit and it cannot be challenged in court.[157] It potentially also breaches Australia's human- rights commitments. Refugees and asylum-seekers have already experienced highly traumatic events. Many have been persecuted in their homeland and face further persecution if they return. Often, they have spent lengthy periods living in refugee camps overseas where they have lived in conditions most of us would easily view as appalling. Many of their children were either born in their homeland or refugee camps. Many of these children only know trauma. Once refugees and asylum-seekers arrive in Australia, they are further traumatised and kept in detention of some kind or on some kind of temporary visa that can be revoked at any time. This can only increase their stress levels and add to their trauma.

Of course, other alternatives would allow them to live in the community once assessed that they are not a security risk, but these are not politically palatable to the two main Australian political parties. Fortunately, once people are free to live in the community, either under a temporary visa or resettled under Australia's Humanitarian Program, the community can support and be with them on their healing journey. Let's look at one or two examples of this healing process in action.

Biloela and the Nadesalingam Family

For many, there is a struggle to pronounce Biloela. Simply, the English pronunciation of the town in Queensland is Bi-luh-wee-luh.

Biloela is in Central Queensland, about 125 kilometres inland from the port of Gladstone and has a population of 5,371. It is the administrative centre for the Shire of Banana. Really, you couldn't find a more quintessentially Australian name for a region. Bananas are a major agricultural crop in Australia, and an antiquated term for a person from Queensland is a "banana bender".

The town of Biloela has become synonymous with the asylum-seeker debate in Australia due to the events surrounding the town and the Nadesalingam family.[158]

Their story is one of high drama. It features legal battles, political intervention, the trauma of detention for families and children, mid-flight court challenges and finally, victory for the family and their supporters. At the heart is the human story of one family fighting an unjust system and a community wrapping themselves around the family as one of their own.

Priya Nadaraja arrived by boat in Australia in 2012, and Nades Murugappan also by boat in 2013. Both claimed asylum from the persecution they feared they would receive if they returned to Sri Lanka. They met in immigration detention, and in 2014 they were married. The couple were relocated to Biloela on bridging visas. Nades found work in the local meat-processing plant, and Priya undertook voluntary work. They became a much-loved part of the local community. Although known to Australian officials as the Murugappan family, they prefer to be known as the Nadesalingam family. This is Nade's full first name, and it is cultural practice for his family to be known by that name.

The couple had two children while living in Biloela. Kopika was born in May 2015 and Tharnicca in 2017.

Unfortunately for them, their bridging visa expired in 2018 and the government of the day refused to renew it. Consequently, they were removed from their home in a dawn raid by immigration officials and taken to the Broadmeadows Detention Centre in Melbourne. Tharnicca celebrated both her first and second birthdays in this detention centre.

The manner of their removal from their home in Biloela distressed members of the local community, and they commenced a strong grassroots campaign to have the family released and returned to their new home of Biloela. The "Home to Bilo" campaign was extremely vocal and attracted national media attention to the family's plight. I doubt the campaign organisers knew how long and hard the campaign would be.

Throughout the campaign, the Department of Home Affairs maintained that processes had been correctly followed, the family did not meet Australia's protection obligations and that they would need to be deported from Australia. The government stuck to their policy that no asylum-seeker arriving by boat would be able to remain in Australia.

In June 2018, the Federal Court rejected the family's appeal against deportation. The court found that the process undertaken by the Immigration Department in rejecting their claim for refugee status had been conducted according to the guidelines set down for these matters. Similarly, in May 2019, their application to have their matter reviewed by the High Court was denied.

On August 29, 2019, the family were placed on a plane. Their destination was to be Sri Lanka. However, a last-minute court injunction stopped the flight mid-air, with the plane landing in Darwin and the family being relocated to Christmas Island. The government closed the detention centre on Christmas Island in October 2018, only for it to be reopened to house the family.[159]

The Prime Minister, Scott Morrison, ruled out ministerial intervention in the family's case. He had been the Immigration Minister in an earlier government that had taken a strong line in stopping people from arriving by boat.

In October 2019, the United Nations Human Rights Committee requested Australia review the family's case and release them from detention.

The grassroots campaign had lost none of its momentum and was continuing to lobby the government to return the family to Biloela.

Things took another dramatic turn for the family in June 2021 when Tharnicca was medically evacuated to Perth with a suspected blood infection. Her mother accompanied her, but her father and sister were not permitted to join them. Of course, this separation gained media attention and further antagonised the grassroots campaign. A week later, her father and sister were flown to Perth for the family to reunite.

The Immigration Minister intervened and placed the family in community detention in Perth. This type of detention is often used while people wait for bridging visas to be issued, but instead of living in a detention centre, they live in a house or a unit and have minimal freedoms. Under community detention, the person has no choice where they live. They are not issued a visa and cannot work. They are provided with a small payment to pay for necessities. While they can leave the unit or house, they cannot travel interstate and need authority to stay somewhere else overnight. They also need authority to have visitors stay overnight. While in community detention, a person is allocated a case worker they must regularly meet with. In short, their liberties are severely curtailed.[160] However, following a change of government in the 2022 election, the Acting Immigration Minister, Dr Jim Chalmers, intervened and granted all four members of the family bridging visas. This meant they could return to Biloela.

The Sunday after their return, Tharnicca celebrated her fifth birthday. This was the first time she could celebrate a birthday in her home town of Biloela. Finally, in August 2022, the family were granted permanent visas.

It is a long story that highlights the power of community in supporting those suffering trauma and using "people power" to fight against unjust decisions. The parents had already experienced trauma before deciding to seek asylum in Australia. They were then placed in mandatory detention—another traumatising experience. But they found each other and then found a loving community to support them in healing from their traumatic experiences. They became valued members of a community and established their family in that same community, only to have all this security taken away in a dawn raid by Immigration officials and placed, once again, in detention. This time it was not only the adult members of the family being placed in a traumatic position, but also their two young children.

These types of traumatic events continued for the family for four years before some compassion was shown and they were released back to their home and supportive community to once again continue their healing journey.

The Home to Bilo campaign is still working to advocate for other asylum-seekers and for changes to the Australian approach to treating asylum-seekers and refugees.

Cairns African Association

Cairns is a growing regional centre in Far North Queensland. In 2022, it had an estimated population of 172,272.

For many, it is known for its natural beauty and access to the Great Barrier Reef and the Wet Tropics. Due to these features, it attracts a large number of both domestic and international tourists. The city also serves as the regional service centre to much of Australia's Far North, providing services and support to many other communities in the Cape York Peninsula. Although known for its tourism, the largest employer in the city is the healthcare and social assistance sector of the economy. This sector employs 16% of the population.

The city prides itself on diversity and is listed as part of the Welcoming Cities network. This is a network of local government areas that value cultural diversity and aim to make their communities a place where all are welcome to equitably participate in the city's cultural, economic, social and civic life. 22% of the population of Cairns was born overseas. 14.1% of the population use a language other than English at home, with 77 different languages spoken. Each year, over 900 residents of Cairns become Australian citizens. The multicultural community is very active, holding frequent festivals and gatherings to celebrate the many cultures represented in the community.

Each year, Cairns welcomes many new residents who are refugees. One of the growing communities is the African Community. The *Settlement Cities Report* published by the Edmund Rice Centre (2022) found that ethno-specific community associations provided much-needed supports to new arrivals and helped them to settle into their new community.[161] These community associations perform a number of roles, such as supporting new arrivals to settle into a new community with different cultural mores, norms and expectations, building community and social cohesion among the new arrivals through celebrations and cultural and/or religious events, and acting as a link between community services and government agencies to assist new arrivals to settle into their new community.[162]

One such ethno-specific community association is the Cairns African Association.

It aims to provide a support network to newly arrived refugees and immigrants from Africa. The association works to assist members in accessing services and aims for its members to develop a spirit of community in their chosen new home. They also want to increase awareness in the greater community about issues directly facing new arrivals from Africa, such as language barriers, social integration, cultural differences and the expectations of the Australian community. Additionally, the association is working to provide cultural and sporting activities for children and young people from Africa along with greater opportunities for connection to each other and the wider community through cultural events and activities.

The association conducts several youth programs to provide opportunities for social interaction, learning, skill-building and the sharing of their different African cultures with both other young African people and the greater community, so that all can learn from one another.

Another important program is Maisha Bora. This program provides essential support for African families. It revolves around many activities to create safe and inclusive spaces for families to come together and further build a sense of community, social cohesion and healing from past trauma, and to cushion the impact of living in a new country with different cultural expectations.

The President of the Cairns African Association is Anna Wairimu Jones, who coordinates the Maisha Bora program. I first met Anna in 2021 when she approached the Communities for Children program in Cairns South to conduct a specific program for African youth to create positive relationships in the Australian cultural environment.

Anna has vast experience working in Australia and many African communities in the area of health promotion and education. The program she proposed was based on a similar one she had conducted in South Africa with border-jumping migrants both from and within the region. She had modified the program to suit the young African people from Cairns. The aim was to work with them on building positive and caring relationships with others, particularly potential romantic and sexual partners. Of particular concern was the difference between the cultural expectations of some of their traditional patriarchal cultural practices and the Australian cultural expectation of gender equality.

This was a lively program. One or two sessions were conducted in the building where I was working. The young people participated in training workshops for the first part of the program. These were then followed by a communal meal that another Cairns African Association member prepared. The communal meal was a joyous occasion with loud, hip-hop music played through a Bluetooth speaker while the young people ate, laughed and generally had a great time getting to know each other. The final day of the program was even more celebratory. Some of the young people had been writing and creating their own music. They had even adopted stage names such as Superboy. The day concluded with a spontaneous concert and African dance display by the young people for the program's organisers and anyone else working in the community centre at the time.

Following the success of this program, Anna approached the Communities for Children program again for further funding. The next project focused on physical activity and cultural exchange between the young African people and the local Indigenous community.

The physical activity component of the program was based at the local Police Citizens Youth Club (PCYC). These sessions aimed to provide the young people with structured physical activity and introduced them to the PCYC as an option for future exercise.

The cultural exchange component involved time spent with an Indigenous organisation on their traditional lands. This was a particularly important component of the program as it introduced the young Africans to local Indigenous practices and culture, adding to their understanding and respect of different cultures. It also provided the potential for reducing tensions between local Indigenous and African youth. This was another successful program.

The next year, Anna approached the Communities for Children program for a small amount of funding to transport a team of young Africans to attend a soccer competition outside the region. The Cairns African Association had been working with African families and youth to create an African soccer team. This was part of their ongoing youth programs. Transport to the competition enabled the young people to see the culmination of their hard work in attending training sessions and building their team. This action built stronger social cohesion between families and youth in the African Community.

Anna and the Cairns African Association have continued to develop the activities and programs they offer members of the local African community. The most recent program is Maisha Bora Resilient Journeys. This program is designed to address the trauma that many African immigrants and resettled refugees confront. Many association members have experienced trauma in their home country, in refugee camps, and in attempting to find a place to offer them a fresh start. Some have experienced extreme poverty, seen their homeland torn apart by violence, had loved ones lost to war or violence and risked everything to find a safe place to live. Many younger members were born in refugee camps and only knew overcrowded and unsafe places as their homes for lengthy periods of time. For some, this has been their entire childhood experience.

Some association members want to address their trauma and start on the path to healing, but they don't know where and how to start. Others are afraid to open up to others about their experiences or want to move on and forget the past, but they find themselves stuck in it. The association has worked hard to design a program where African community members can gather once a week in a safe, inclusive space where they and their families can start to build a community. This provides an opportunity for people to get to know each other, share their different cultures and build enough trust to be in a position where they feel safe enough to open up about their traumatic past. As we have said before, healing from trauma happens in the community in those small opportunities to share just enough so that the person still feels safe and unashamed about their experience. It is one brief conversation at a time, one moment of having the strength to share that moves us on in our healing journey. This not only has dividends for the person sharing their story, but it also creates a deeper bond of trust between them and those they have chosen to share with.

Healing from trauma is not the only benefit the program offers. While structured sessions with mentors to assist in opening up about trauma is part of the program, there is so much more on offer. To create a strong and cohesive community, other activities are scheduled to support people and their families to build connections with others in a non-threatening environment.

Just as the community of Biloela extended the offer of friendship and support to strangers in a strange land and welcomed them into the town to be part of what Biloela represents, the Cairns African Association is doing the same thing for African immigrants in Cairns. Each time the offer to be part of our communities is extended to another, our community benefits and we provide an opportunity for fellowship, healing and safety to another. And after all, isn't that what community is really all about?

CONCLUSION:

Trauma and Community— A Part of Our Lives

Trauma can happen to any one of us at any time. When it does, it is not our fault. We are not to blame. It just happens and it can scar us deeply. When we are hit by trauma, we can respond to it in many ways. Often, our responses are not positive or healing. They are often detrimental. Again, we are not to blame for our trauma. While not excusing some of the damaging behaviours that we exhibit in response to trauma, they are not our core problem. In many ways, these self-destructive, angry, abusive, violent and unhelpful behaviours are the symptoms of something much more profound.

But the good news is that just as trauma is part of our lives, healing from it is also part of our lives. Without the support of a strong and cohesive community (our crew), the healing will not occur. Just as a drive for social connection is part of who we are as a species, so is healing as a community. Nature and evolution have provided us with a brain that never stops changing and rewiring itself to come to terms with our changing world. This capacity to never stop learning is an essential part of who we are as humans, and together, we can support each other to be the best we can ever be.

While trauma is part of our human experience, we can do so much to reduce the opportunity for it to occur. We have seen how exposure to adverse childhood experiences (ACEs) can change how the brain develops and result in future adverse outcomes. And while the aim is to prevent ACEs, this may always be not possible. But intervention at any time can have an impact and rewire the brain so that the effect of ACEs on the brain is lessened and healing commenced.

We also know that resilience mitigates the impact of ACEs (i.e., individual and community resilience offers protection from the harmful impacts of ACEs, allowing both the brain and body to start healing). We have seen how trauma can happen at any time in our lives. It can potentially impact our health and wellbeing. The development of trusted adult relationships, having supportive friends and being engaged in community activities can be significant factors in our healing journey.

Community connection with others plays a major role in healing from ACEs and associated trauma, and in maintaining our wellbeing. It is amazing how our brains retain plasticity throughout our lives and continue to change in relation to our experiences and environment. We never stop learning and have the potential to never stop healing. Having a caring community around us is at the core of this healing journey. Without this community, healing (if it does occur) will be slower and a much more difficult task.

We have been on a lengthy journey together. We visited trauma, the healing power of communities and what they look like in action. We examined some of the big questions we all have about crime, families, the impact of disasters on people, and the important concept of welcoming the stranger.

Now, we have returned to trauma and community. Because this is what we really want. To be healed from our trauma and pain. And community is where we heal.

APPENDIX:

Ideas to Connect with Your Neighbours

Say Hi: Smile, wave and say hello to people in your neighbourhood.

Introduction Time: Introduce your children to your neighbours. If they become trusted friends, your children will feel safe to go to them in an emergency.

Lemonade Time: Buy lemonade, eggs, or whatever children are selling at their street stalls.

Let's Walk: Ask if your neighbour would like to join you for a walk with you and your children.

A Fence Shouldn't Divide Us: Give children's stray balls (or drones!) back.

Who Needs a Babysitter?: Connect with neighbourhood teenagers and offer them babysitting opportunities.

School Pickup: Offer to help with school runs if your children are at school together.

Let's Celebrate: Celebrate special-event days with your neighbours and organise events like an Easter egg hunt, Santa to visit or Halloween trick-or-treat.

The Game: Set up a cricket, soccer or football game in the local park and invite your neighbours.

Free Library: Start a street library – more info here: www. streetlibrary.org.au.

Pet Sitter: Offer to look after your neighbour's pets while they are away.

Crop Swap: Share produce from your garden.

Recipe Time: Swap a favourite recipe with a neighbour and share the delight.

Tinkering About: Spend more time in your front yard as a simple way to connect with nearby neighbours and those passing by.

Cuppa: Organise a 'cuppa by the kerb' where you invite your neighbours to bring a cuppa and have a chat in the street together at a set time.

Street Party: Organise a street party.

BBQ Time: Invite your neighbours over for a barby.

The Big Match: Invite your neighbours over to watch a footy game or any other sport.

Dinner's Ready!: Have a progressive dinner where everyone prepares a course.

Bin Night: Take in your neighbour's garbage bin.

Mail: Offer to collect the mail while your neighbour is away.

Tools: Share resources (e.g., garden tools, lawnmowers).

Christmas Time: Drop a Christmas card in your neighbours' letterboxes.

Nothing to See Here: Keep an eye on your neighbour's house and pop over if you see anything unusual.

Be Helpful: Offer to help a neighbour with shopping or small, odd jobs. If there is a blackout, check in on an elderly neighbour and see if they have a torch handy.

Meals on Wheels: Deliver a meal if your neighbour has been unwell.

Bake-Off: Organise a bake-off and cake tasting.

Spread the News: Let your neighbours know you are having a party, garage sale, or other event – perhaps invite them! Keep them in the loop.

We Need to Talk: Talk through small issues before they become big problems.

Volunteer: Check if there are volunteering opportunities at a local school or sports club.

The Roaming Gnome: A street gnome that roams the street. If the gnome ends up in your yard, it is your turn to relocate him in the neighbourhood.

Cubby Building: Bring local children together to build a cubby together or visit each other's cubby houses.

Who has the Best Letterbox?: Have a street project to dress up letterboxes around different themes – Halloween, Christmas, Harmony Week, etc.

Happy Birthday: Have a birthday party for your street. It does not have to be a true date, just choose a date and each year that date becomes your street's birthday.

Oh Christmas Tree: Decorate a significant tree in your street and dedicate it to be a street Christmas tree.

Walking School Bus: If your street is within walking distance of the local school, gather parents and kids from your neighbourhood to walk to school as a group, creating a walking school bus.

Decorating Competitions: Decorate your front verandah and post it on Instagram. Check out your neighbours' decorations and start conversations about them. This could be for Halloween, Christmas or any other celebratory occasion.

Car Wash: Set up an area for the children in the street to wash your neighbours' cars. Letterbox-drop to invite people along.

Street Project: Develop a community project for your whole street. Examples: build bird feeders for the trees in your street, a street library or a street seat.

Light Show: Put fairy lights in trees in your front yard and invite your neighbours to do the same. You can even host a get-together under the lights once they are up.

Photography Competition and/or Exhibition: Invite your neighbours to take photos of the things they love about their street. Exhibit the photos in the street and ask your locally elected member or other person of interest to judge. Request a donated prize from a local business. Host a celebration for the competition.

Listening Bench: Set up a bench seat, put up a sign and call it the street listening booth. Take some time out to listen to your neighbours' stories.

Morning Tea: Get together with your neighbours and plan a roaming morning tea with a different neighbour hosting each month and everyone bringing a plate of food to share.

Book Club: Start up a book club by inviting your neighbours along for an afternoon tea. Take turns choosing a book to read. Meet as often as it suits you and your neighbours.

Movie Night: Set up the TV (or projector if someone has one), chairs and blankets, make popcorn and have a family movie night. Families can bring a picnic dinner, drinks and snacks.

History Tour: If a resident knows about the history of your area, they can lead a walking tour for all the newer residents.

House Concert: Gather your talented musicians, singers or poets for performance nights in each other's backyards or homes. BYO drinks and shared food.

Art Show: Showcase the street's artistic talent with a local exhibition in your home, apartment or laneway.

Street Art: Get some boxes of chalk and ask your neighbours and their children to decorate your street footpaths with images and welcoming messages.

Neighbour Happy Hour: Have a weekly 'happy hour' where whoever is free drops in to say hello at a designated house or front porch. This may or may not include having a drink – it's more about being social.

Treasure Hunt: Organise a street treasure hunt – finish with a BBQ.

Grown-Ups Only: Create a mothers' or fathers' group to have a regular social gathering, with or without kids.

Games in the Park: Make a regular time for parents and kids to meet at the park to play games together.

Homework Club: Start a homework club where children can do their homework together and help each other.

Ice-Cream Party: Organise a street ice-cream party. Each household brings a different-flavoured tub of ice-cream to share. Don't let it melt!

Lego Building: Put a blanket and some boxes of Lego in the front yard and invite your neighbours to come and build with Lego. Remember, no one is ever too old to build with Lego so don't just invite neighbours with children.

Random Acts of Kindness: Encourage your children to do random acts of kindness for others in the street, particularly the elderly or those who live on their own, as well as new residents.

Star Light, Star Bright: Bring your children out into the street or front yards to do stargazing.

Talent Quest: Organise a street talent show – everyone brings refreshments and children get to demonstrate their talents in front of an encouraging crowd.

Street Garage/Yard Sale: Invite all your neighbours to come together for a combined garage/yard sale on the same day. Check out for inspiration and resources. (https://www.garage-saletrail.com.au).

Job Sharing: "I will mow your lawn this month, you mow mine next month" or "I mow your lawn in exchange for you doing something different for me."

Share Phone Numbers: Give your number to your neighbours.

Neighbour Day: Run a neighbour day event each year (e.g., at the end of March) and invite all the new and old neighbours together via a letterbox drop (https://neighbourday.org).

Social media: Create a closed street Facebook or Instagram group. Invite your neighbours to join via a letterbox drop. Use the group to share ideas, swap items or services and generally support each other.[163]

Endnotes

1   National Institute for the Clinical Application for Behavioral Medicine, *How a Caregiver's Trauma Can Impact a Child's Development* www.nicabm. com/how-a-caregivers-trauma-can-impact-a-childs-development-info-graphic/

2   Symons, Rachel, *Adverse Childhood Experiences* Presentation

3   Ibid

4   Ibid

5   Bramley, Ellie Violet, *The Trauma Doctor: Gabor Maté on happiness, hope and how to heal our deepest wounds,* The Guardian April 13 2023

6   PACES Connection, *Understanding ACEs* https://www.pacesconnection. com/pages/handouts Patterson, C., & Barrie, L (2023)

7   Ibid

8   PACES Connection, *3 Realms of ACEs* https://www.pacesconnection. com/pages/handouts Patterson, C., & Barrie, L (2023)

9   Ibid

10 Felitti V.J., Anda R.F., Nordenberg D., Williamson D.F., Spitz A.M., Edwards V., Koss M.P., Marks J.S. *Relationship of childhood abuse and household dysfunction to many of the leading causes of death in adults. The Adverse Childhood Experiences (ACE) Study.* National Library of Medicine. https://pubmed.ncbi.nlm.nih.gov/9635069/

11 Cited in Di Lemma L.C.G., Davies A.R., Ford K., Hughes K., Homolova L., Gray B and Richardson G. (2019). *Responding to Adverse Childhood Experiences: An evidence review of interventions to prevent and address adversity across the life course.* Public Health Wales, Cardiff and Bangor University, Wrexham

12 CDC Vital Signs, *Adverse Childhood experiences (ACEs)—Preventing early trauma to improve adult health,* Centers for Disease Control and Prevention https://www.cdc.gov/vitalsigns/aces/pdf/vs-1105-aces-H.pdf

13 PACES Connection, *Understanding ACEs* https://www.pacesconnection. com/pages/handouts Patterson, C., & Barrie, L (2023)

14 Impact Services Corporation and New Kensington Community Development Corporation (2020), *Connected Community: A Trauma-In-formed Community Engagement Curriculum* p.4

15 Perry, B., Winfrey O., (2021) *Whatever Happened to You*, p.177, Flatiron Books New York

16 Aces Too High, https://acestoohigh.com/aces-101/ Alberta Wellness Initiative, *The Brain Story* (accessed on 19 April 2023). This page provides links to a number of research articles on PCEs.

17 Ibid

18 Ibid

19 Perry, B and Winfrey, O. (2021) *What Happened to You*, p.67, Flatiron Books, New York

20 Westoboy,P., Palmer, D., Lathouras, A. (2020) *40 Critical Thinkers in Community Development*, p.20, Rugby U.K.: Practical Action Publishing

21 Lim, M. *Australian Loneliness Report: A survey exploring the loneliness levels of Australians and the impact on their health and wellbeing*, p.24, Swinburne University of Technology

22 Ibid, p.20

23 Perry, B and Winfrey, O. (2021) *What Happened to You*, p.171, Flatiron Books, New York

24 Perry, B and Winfrey, O. (2021) *What Happened to You*, p.177, Flatiron Books, New York

25 Russell, C. & McKnight, J. (2022) *The Connected Community: Discovering the Health, Wealth, and Power of Neighbourhoods*, pp.85–100, Berrett-Koehler Publishers, Inc.

26 Ibid

27 Seppala, E., (2014), *Connectedness & Health: The Science of Social Connection*, Stanford University Centre for Compassion and Altruism Research and Education https://ccare.stanford.edu/uncategorized/connectedness-health-the-science-of-social-connection-infographic/

28 Ibid, p.90

29 Livingstone, Rhonda, (2018), *It Takes a Village to Raise a Child: The Role of Community—Part 2* ACECQA https://www.acecqa.gov.au/latest-news/blog/it-takes-village-raise-child-role-community-part-2

30 Ibid

31 Russell, C. & McKnight, J. (2022) *The Connected Community: Discovering the Health, Wealth, and Power of Neighbourhoods*, pp.95–97, Berrett-Koehler Publishers, Inc.

32 Diers, Jim (2019) *You Can't Build Community Without Doing The Bump* https://abcdinaction.org/jim-diers/blog/251/you-cant-build-community-without-doing-the-bump

33 Patterson C., & Barrie L. (2023) https://theconversation.com/forget-the-conspiracies-15-ninute-cities-will-free-us-to-improve-our-mental-health-and-wellbeing-200823

34 Ibid

35 Tait, B., (2020) https://www.forbes.com/sites/forbescoachescouncil/2020/03/11/traditional-leadership-vs-servant-leadership/?sh=68816393451e

36 Block, P., (2018), *Community: The Structure of Belonging*, p.89, Berrett-Koehler Publishers, Inc.

37 Russell, C. & McKnight, J (2022), *The Connected Community: Discovering the Health, Wealth and Power of Neighbourhoods*, p.64, Berrett-Koehler Publishers, Inc.

38 Ibid, p.69

39 Foundation for Intentional Community https://www.ic.org/foundation-for-intentional-community/

40 L'Arche Australia https://www.larche.org.au/about-us/the-larche-story-in-australia/

41 Ibid

42 Collective Impact Forum & FSG, *Backbone Starter Guide: A Summary of Major Resources about the Backbone*, pp.8–9 https://collectiveimpactforum.org/wp-content/uploads/2021/12/Backbone-Starter-Guide.pdf

43 O. Dowd, C. https://www.caraodowd.com/lockdownlocalsbook

44 Pyne, Rob. https://www.robpyne.com.au/

45 Perry, B and Winfrey, O. (2021) *What Happened to You*, p.101, Flatiron Books, New York

46 Ibid

47 Eaton, M., and Utting, A. *Queensland tops nation for child detention and youth repeat offenders, Productivity Commission data reveals* https://www.abc.net.au/news/2023-01-24/qld-youth-detention-figures-show-high-recidivist-rate/101886998

48 Queensland Government, https://www.qld.gov.au/law/sentencing-prisons-and-probation/young-offenders-and-the-justice-system/sentencing-young-offenders/youth-court-orders/supervised-release-orders

49 Queensland Government, https://www.qld.gov.au/law/sentencing-prisons-and-probation/young-offenders-and-the-justice-system/sentencing-young-offenders/youth-court-orders/intensive-supervision-orders

50 Smee, Ben *Queensland youth justice minister denounced policies now spruiked as 'toughest in the nation'*, The Guardian, 12 June 2023

51 Smee, Ben *Evidence refutes claims of youth crime wave, former Queensland children's court boss says*, The Guardian, 9 March 2023

52 Scottish Government (2018), *Understanding Childhood Adversity, Resilience and Crime* https://www.gov.scot/binaries/content/documents/govscot/publications/research-and-analysis/2018/05/understanding-childhood-adversity-resilience-crime/documents/00535550-pdf/00535550-pdf/govscot%3Adocument/00535550.pdf

53 Ibid

54 Ibid

55 Eaton, M., and Utting, A. *Queensland tops nation for child detention and youth repeat offenders, Productivity Commission data reveals* https://www.abc.net.au/news/2023-01-24/qld-youth-detention-figures-show-high-recidivist-rate/101886998

56 Nembhard, S & Lima, N., (2022) *To Improve Safety, Understanding and Addressing the Link between Childhood Trauma and Crime Is Key*, Urban Institute https://www.urban.org/urban-wire/improve-safety-understanding-and-addressing-link-between-childhood-trauma-and-crime-key

57 EMDR Institute, Inc. https://www.emdr.com/what-is-emdr/

58 Scottish Government (2018), *Understanding Childhood Adversity, Resilience and Crime* https://www.gov.scot/binaries/content/documents/govscot/publications/research-and-analysis/2018/05/understanding-childhood-adversity-resilience-crime/documents/00535550-pdf/00535550-pdf/govscot%3Adocument/00535550.pdf

59 Ibid

60 RMIT Centre for Innovative Justice, *What is Restorative Justice?* https://cij.org.au/opencircle/what-is-restorative-justice/

61 Chief Mis'el Joe, Vaandering, D.,, Ricciardelli, R., Sulaimon, G., Moore S., (2022), *Two Eared Listening is Essential for Understanding Restorative Justice in Canada*, The Conversation

62 Malotane Henkeman, S (2016), *Why a narrow view of restorative justice blunts its impact*, The Conversation

63 Block, P., (2018), *Community: The Structure of Belonging*, p.54, Berrett-Koehler Publishers, Inc.

64 Malotane Henkeman, S (2016), *Why a narrow view of restorative justice blunts its impact*, The Conversation

65 Birdsong ,Mia, (2020), *How We Show Up: Reclaiming Family, Friendship and Community*, Hachette Book Group

66 Perry, B and Winfrey, O. (2021) *What Happened to You*, p.180, Flatiron Books, New York

67 Leigh, Andrew (2023), *Rebuilding Communities in a Friendship Recession*, The Daily Telegraph

68 Daley, J (2018) *The U.K. Now Has a 'Minister for Loneliness'. Here's Why It Matters*, Smithsonian Magazine

69 Ibid

70 Perry, B and Winfrey, O. (2021) *What Happened to You*, p.177, Flatiron Books, New York

71 Putnam, Robert, D. (2000), *Bowling Alone: The Collapse and Revival of American Community*, p.19, Simon & Schuster New York.

72 Ibid, pp.314–315

73 Russell, C (2016) *Taking a Strengths-based Approach to Young People: Moving from 'at risk' to 'at promise'. Part1* https://www.nurturedevelopment.org/blog/taking-strengths-based-approach-young-people-moving-risk-promise-part-1/

74 Ibid

75 Sanctuary Point Community Pride https://spcp.org.au/

76 Australian Broadcasting Corporation, (2021) *Premier Elect Dominic Perrottet First Public Speech* https://www.abc.net.au/news/2021-10-05/premier-elect-dominic-perrottet-first-public-speech/100514154

77 Lott, T., *Traditional families are not the only preserve of moral values*, The Guardian 26 March, 2016

78 Australian Bureau of Statistics (2016) *Census of Population and Housing: Census Dictionary*

79 State Library of NSW, *Eighteen Years Earlier* www.sl.nsw.gov.au/learning/journey-first-fleet/eighteen-years-earlier#:

80 Ibid

81 Ibid

82 Rule of Law Education Centre, *Terra Nullius* https://www.ruleoflaw.org.au/education/australian-colonies/terra-nullius/

83 Ibid

84 Ibid

85 Australian Academy of the Humanities (2023) *The Australian Wars: new insights from a digital map* https://humanities.org.au/power-of-the-humanities/the-australian-wars-new-insights-from-a-digital-map/

86 Ibid

87 Ibid

88 Australian Human Rights Commission (1997), *Bringing Them Home Report*, p.22, https://humanrights.gov.au/sites/default/files/content/pdf/social_justice/bringing_them_home_report.pdf

89 Guthrie, J., et al, (2020) '*The answers were there before white man come in': stories of strength and resilience for responding to violence in Aboriginal and Torres Strait Islander communities*—Family and Community Safety for Aboriginal and Torres Strait Islander Peoples Study Report, p.37

90 Halliwell, Celeste., *Parenting from Western and Traditional Indigenous Perspectives*, Building Brains Together https://www.buildingbrains.ca/blog/b2nwoc4y58ml5lsxnw8u6f8vjuknra

91 Queensland Government, *The Meaning of Family in Aboriginal and Torres Strait Islander Cultures* https://cspm.csyw.qld.gov.au/practice-kits/safe-care-and-connection/working-with-aboriginal-and-torres-strait-islander/seeing-and-understanding/the-meaning-of-family-in-aboriginal-and-torres-str

92 Perry, B and Winfrey, O. (2021) *What Happened to You*, p.220, Flatiron Books, New York

93 Queensland Government, *About Foster Care* www.qld.gov.au/community/caring-child/foster-kinship-care/foster-kinship-care-about

94 Moore, T.G., Arefadib, N., Deery, A., & West, S. (2017). *The First Thousand Days: An Evidence Paper*. Parkville, Victoria; Centre for Community Child Health, Murdoch Children's Research Institute

95 Kinsella, M., and Monk, C., (2009) *Impact of Maternal Stress, Depression & Anxiety on Fetal Neurobehavioral Development* Clinical Obstetrics and Gynecology

96 Ibid.

97 McLean, S., (2019) *Understanding the Impacts of Fetal Alcohol Spectrum Disorder (FASD) on Child Mental Health* Emerging Minds, South Australia

98 Kinsella, M., and Monk, C., (2009) *Impact of Maternal Stress, Depression & Anxiety on Fetal Neurobehavioral Development* Clinical Obstetrics and Gynecology

99 Moore, T.G., Arefadib, N., Deery, A., & West, S. (2017). *The First Thousand Days: An Evidence Paper,* p.5, Parkville, Victoria; Centre for Community Child Health, Murdoch Children's Research Institute

100 Ibid, p.6

101 Ibid

102 Ngamumu https://www.ngamumu.com/

103 Pulley, Roz (2017), *Program helps Cairns dads and builds stronger families* Cairns Post February 22

104 Office of the Surgeon General (2023) Our *Epidemic of Loneliness and Isolation: The U.S. Surgeon General's Advisory on the Healing Effects of Social Connection and Community*

105 Lim, M. *Australian Loneliness Report: A survey exploring the loneliness levels of Australians and the impact on their health and wellbeing,* Swinburne University of Technology

106 Office of the Surgeon General (2023) Our *Epidemic of Loneliness and Isolation: The U.S. Surgeon General's Advisory on the Healing Effects of Social Connection and Community,* p.8

107 Ibid, p.8

108 Ibid, p.9

109 Lim, M. *Australian Loneliness Report: A survey exploring the loneliness levels of Australians and the impact on their health and wellbeing,* p.5 Swinburne University of Technology

110 Office of the Surgeon General (2023) Our *Epidemic of Loneliness and Isolation: The U.S. Surgeon General's Advisory on the Healing Effects of Social Connection and Community* p.13

111 Ibid

112 Ibid

113 Leigh, Andrew (2023), *Rebuilding Communities in a Friendship Recession,* The Daily Telegraph

114 Office of the Surgeon General (2023) Our *Epidemic of Loneliness and Isolation: The U.S. Surgeon General's Advisory on the Healing Effects of Social Connection and Community* p.16

115 Ibid, pp.24–25

116 Ibid, p.26

117 Lim, M. *Australian Loneliness Report: A survey exploring the loneliness levels of Australians and the impact on their health and wellbeing,* Swinburne University of Technology

118 Office of the Surgeon General (2023) Our *Epidemic of Loneliness and Isolation: The U.S. Surgeon General's Advisory on the Healing Effects of Social Connection and Community* pp.24–30

119 Ibid, p.32

[120] De Jong, E., (2023), *The kindness of acquaintances is important in recovering from a mental health crisis*, The Guardian 31 July

[121] Office of the Surgeon General (2023) *Our Epidemic of Loneliness and Isolation: The U.S. Surgeon General's Advisory on the Healing Effects of Social Connection and Community* p.33

[122] Ibid, p.34

[123] Ibid, p.39

[124] Ibid, p.40

[125] Relationships Australia *About Neighbour Day* https://neighbourseveryday.org/about-neighbour-day/#RA

[126] Neighbours Every Day https://neighbourseveryday.org/

[127] National Museum of Australia, *Defining Moments: Canberra Bushfires* www.nma.gov.au/defining-moments/resources/canberra-bushfires

[128] The Sydney Morning Herald, *The Anatomy of the Lismore Disaster*, The Sydney Morning Herald, June 30 , 2022

[129] Chenery, S., *The never-ending fallout of the Northern River floods: People are just worn down*, The Guardian, 20 February, 2023 https://www.theguardian.com/australia-news/2023/feb/20/the-never-ending-fallout-of-the-lismore-floods-people-are-just-worn-down

[130] Scott, H., Bosomworth, K., Fuenfgeld H., (2017) *Adaptation for Recovery Evaluation Report for East Gippsland Shire Council*, p.9, Centre for Urban Research, RMIT University, Melbourne

[131] Ibid, p.5

[132] Weinstein, E., Wolin, J., Rose, S. (2014) *Trauma-Informed Community Building: A Model for Strengthening Communities in Trauma-Affected Neighbourhoods*, Bridge Housing and the Health Equity Institute

[133] Ibid, pp. 13–15

[134] Howard, A., Rawsthorne, M., Sampson, D. & Katrak, M. (2020) *Supporting community-led approaches to disaster preparedness: Summary Research Report*, p.3. Foundation for Rural & Regional Renewal and Resilience NSW, University of Sydney and University of Newcastle

[135] Ibid, p.4

[136] Ibid, p.6

[137] Ibid, pp. 7–8

[138] Ibid, pp. 9–10

[139] Block, P., (2018), *Community: The Structure of Belonging*, p.120, Berrett-Koehler Publishers, Inc.

[140] Kentgen, Lisa (2023) *The Practice of Belonging: Six Lessons from Vibrant Communities to Combat Loneliness, Foster Diversity and Cultivate Caring Relationships*, p.145, North Atlantic Books

[141] Ibid, p.148

[142] Profile id: Community Profile Australia https://profile.id.com.au/australia/volunteering

[143] Thelman, J., (2020) *What it means to be a truly welcoming community*, International Institute of New England

144 Immigration Museum, *Journeys to Australia: Celebrate the journeys that changed Australia forever* https://museumsvictoria.com.au/immigrationmuseum/resources/journeys-to-australia/

145 Ibid

146 Ibid

147 Ibid

148 Overseas Migration, Australian Bureau of Statistics https://www.abs.gov.au/statistics/people/population/overseas-migration/latest-release

149 Migration Program Statistics, Australian Bureau of Statistics

150 Immigration Museum, *Journeys to Australia: Celebrate the journeys that changed Australia forever* https://museumsvictoria.com.au/immigrationmuseum/resources/journeys-to-australia/

151 Department of Home Affairs, *Discussion Paper: Australia's Humanitarian Program 2023-24* Australian Government https://www.homeaffairs.gov.au/reports-and-pubs/files/australias-humanitarian-program-23-24-discussion-paper.pdf

152 Spinks, H., McCluskey I., *Asylum-Seekers and the Refugee Convention* Parliamentary Library, Parliament of Australia https://www.aph.gov.au/About_Parliament/Parliamentary_Departments/Parliamentary_Library/pubs/BriefingBook44p/AsylumSeekers#

153 World Vision, *The Refugee Crisis: A Global Issue* https://www.worldvision.com.au/global-issues/work-we-do/refugees/refugees-and-asylum-seekers

154 Ibid

155 Ibid

156 Australian Human Rights Commission (2023) *Immigration Detention and Human Rights* https://humanrights.gov.au/our-work/asylum-seekers-and-refugees/projects/immigration-detention-and-human-rights

157 Ibid

158 Semmler, E., (2022) *The Biloela Tamil asylum-seeker family and their fight for protection in Australia* ABC News https://www.abc.net.au/news/2022-06-10/nadesalingam-biloela-tamil-family-asylum-seeker-explainer/101139388

159 Koziol, M (2018) *After 10 years, the notorious Christmas Island detention centre has quietly closed* https://www.smh.com.au/politics/federal/after-10-years-the-notorious-christmas-island-detention-centre-has-quietly-closed-20181004-p507r0.html

160 De Poloni, G. & Kaur, H. (2021) *What will community detention be like for the Biloela Tamil family in Perth?* ABC News https://www.abc.net.au/news/2021-06-17/what-is-community-detention-biloela-familys-new-life/100220598

161 Edmund Rice Centre, *Settlement Cities: A place-based study of Australia's major centres for refugee resettlement*, p.10 (Edmund Rice Centre, 2022)

162 Ibid, pp.75–76

163 Hambledon House Community Centre, *Neighbour Day 27 March 2022* https://hambledonhouse.com.au/neighbour-day-27-march-2022